Python Programming Illustrated For Beginners & Intermediates:

"Learn By Doing" Approach-Step By Step Ultimate Guide To Mastering Python: The Future Is Here!

I0489975

FREE E-BOOK DOWNLOAD :

http://bit.ly/2yJsyq4

or

http://pragmaticsolutionstech.com/

Use the link above to get instant access to the bestselling E-Book **Data Analytics' Guide For Beginners** completely FREE!

Table of Contents

Chapter 1

Introduction

Python is a loosely typed object oriented programming language used to perform variety of programming tasks ranging from web development and desktop application development to data science and machine learning etc. Owing to its simplicity of syntax and ease of learning, Python has become one of the leading programming languages of the world. Python was created by Guido van Rossum in late 1980s. This book provides a gateway to in-depth Python programming.

Why Python?

There are several advantages of learning Python. Some of them are as follows:

- **Easy to learn**

Python is one of the easiest languages to learn owing to its super simple syntax and loose typing. Unlike other languages, you don't have to learn how to use myriads of bracket types in order specify code blocks.

You also don't get end of line semicolon errors. Finally, you also don't have to specify the type of variable while storing data in it. These points might sound trivial to expert programmers, but for a person new to programming they are serious turn-offs.

- **Open Source and Large Developer Community**

Python is an open source language which means it can be used to develop, share and distribute applications for commercial as well as non-commercial purposes without any copyright infringements. Furthermore, Python's large developer community makes it easier to lookup for solutions to the problem.

- **Support for Web development**

Python can be used for developing websites. In fact there are some very good Python frameworks such as Django and Flask that make server side web development much easier and robust.

- **Used for Data Science Machine Learning**

You would have heard the term "Data is the future." If data is really the future, then Python is surely the language to learn since most of the data science and machine learning are currently being implemented via Python. There are several machine learning and deep learning libraries such as Sklearn, Tensorflow, Keras that made it simple to develop complex machine learning models.

Important Features of Python

Following are some of the most important features of Python:

- **Source code to Byte code**

Python source code is compiled directly to byte code without any intermediate steps. This makes Python script run on multiple platforms without requiring any additional tool.

- **Object Oriented**

Python is 100% object oriented language. Everything in Python is an object. Furthermore, python provides an easy way to create new objects via classes.

- **Support for C/C++ Extension**

Python code can be further extended in C and C++. Speed of a Python program can be significantly increased this way.

- **Dynamic Language**

Python is a dynamic language. Values, instead of variables are bound to types. Furthermore, Method and function lookup is performed at runtime.

- **Automatic Garbage Collection**

Garbage collection is performed automatically in Python. However, "gc" module can be used to perform garbage collection at any given time.

- **Highly Structured Language**

Statements, functions, classes, modules and packages and most importantly Python's indentation based syntax allows developers to write highly structured and readable code.

- **Fast and Maintainable Compared to Other Languages**

In comparison with other compiled languages, Python is faster, more structured and more maintainable.

About the Book

This book is aimed towards providing in-depth yet simple insight into Python programming language. The book is geared towards beginner as well as advanced readers. The book helps beginners get their feet wet with practical Python. On the other hand, it can be used by expert users as a reference to different basic and advanced Python concepts.

All the important Python concepts have been grouped into chapters. A chapter contains theoretical information about particular Python concepts along with their implementation in the form of Python script. To get the most of this book, readers are suggested to first thoroughly understand the concept and then practice the code.

What's next?

In the next chapter we will set up the environment required to run python script. We will install different software needed to run the scripts in this book. Happy Coding!!!

Chapter 2

Environment Setup

In this chapter we will install the software that we are going to use to run our Python programs. There are several options available in this regard. You can simply install core Python and use a text editor like notepad to write Python programs. These programs can then be run via command line utilities. The other option is to install an Integrated Develop Environment (IDE) for Python. IDE provides a complete programming environment including Python installation, Editors and debugging tools. Most of the advanced programmers take the IDE route for Python development. We are also going to take the same route.

Anaconda is the IDE that we are going to use throughout this book. Anaconda is light, easy to install and comes with variety of development tools. Anaconda has its own command line utility to install third party software. And the good thing is that with Anaconda, you don't have to separately install Python environment.

Downloading and Installing Anaconda

Follow these steps to download and install anaconda. In this section we will show the process of installing Anaconda for windows. The installation process remains almost same for Linux and Mac.

1- Go to the following URL https://www.anaconda.com/downlo ad/

2- You will be presented with the following webpage. Select Python 3.6 version as this is currently the latest version of Python. Click the "Download" button to download the executable file. It takes 2-3 minutes to download the file depending upon the speed of your internet.

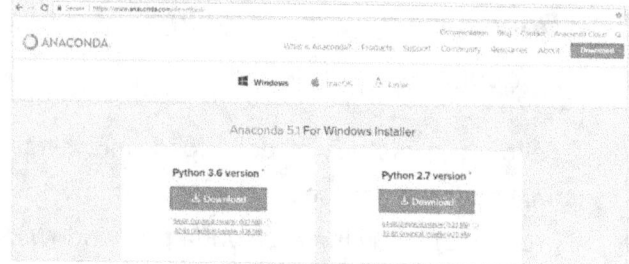

3- Once the executable file is downloaded, go to the download folder and run the executable. The name of the executable file should be similar to "Anaconda3-5.1.0-Windows-x86_64." When you run the file you will see installation wizard like the one in the following screenshot. Click "Next" button.

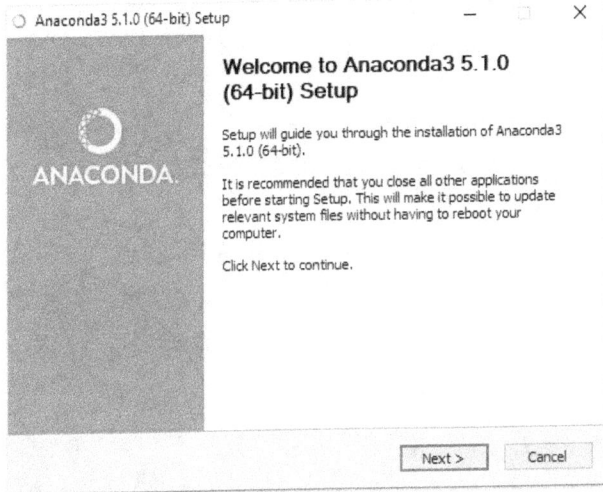

4- "License Agreement" dialogue box will appear. Read the license agreement and Click "I Agree" button.

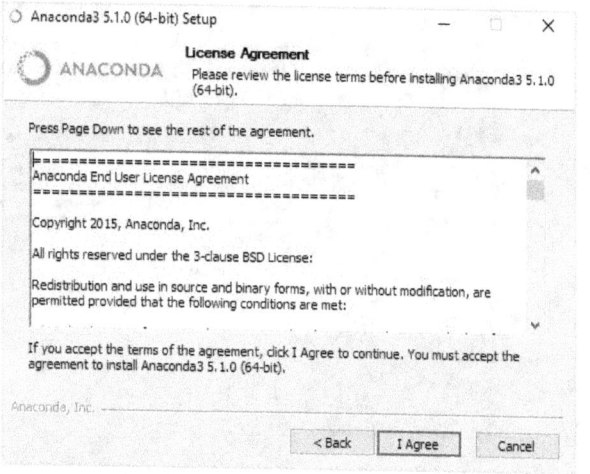

5- From the "Select Installation Type"
dialogue box, check the "Just Me"
radio button and click "Next" button
as shown in the following
screenshot.

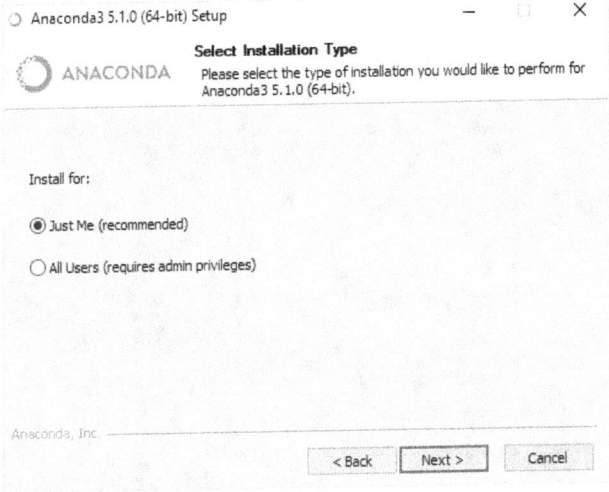

6- Choose the installation directory (Default is preferred) from the "Choose Install Location" dialogue box and click "Next" button. You should have around 3 GB of free space in your installation directory.

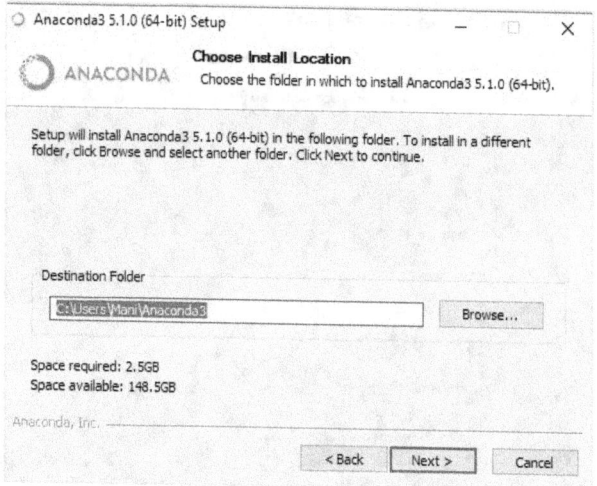

7- From the "Advanced Installation Options" dialogue box, select the second checkbox "Register Anaconda as my default Python 3.6" and click the "Install" button as shown in the following screenshot.

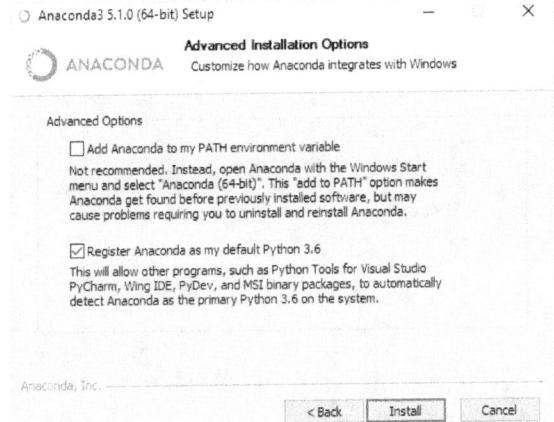

The installation process will start which can take some time to complete. Sit back and enjoy a cup of coffee.

8- Once the installation completes, click the "Next" button as shown below.

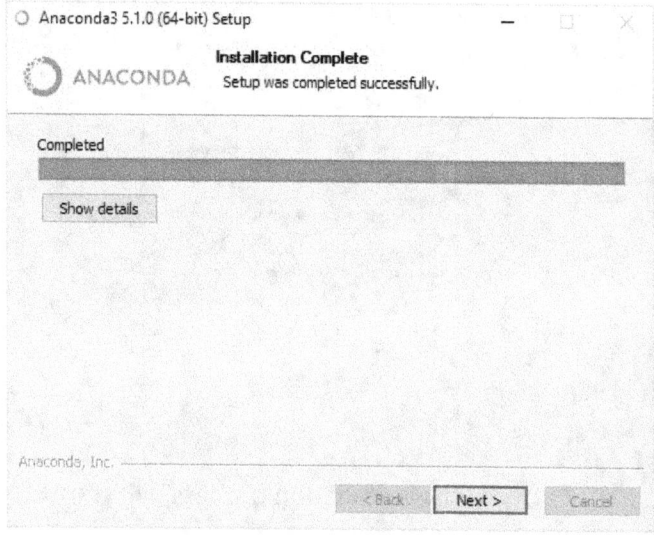

9- "Microsoft Visual Studio Code
Installation" window appear, click
"Skip" button.

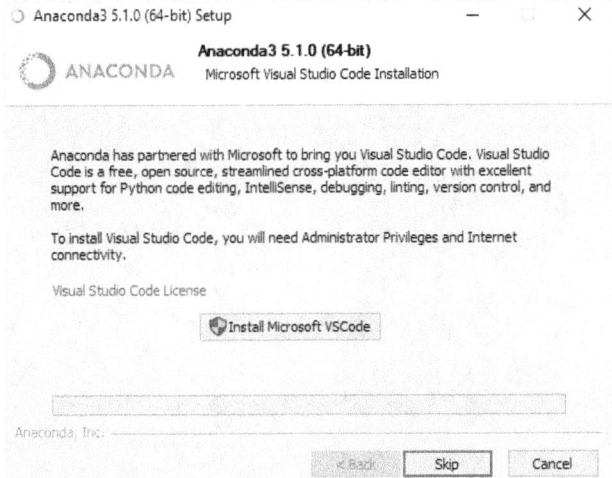

10- Congratulations, you have installed Anaconda. Uncheck the both the checkboxes on the dialogue box that appears and "Finish" button.

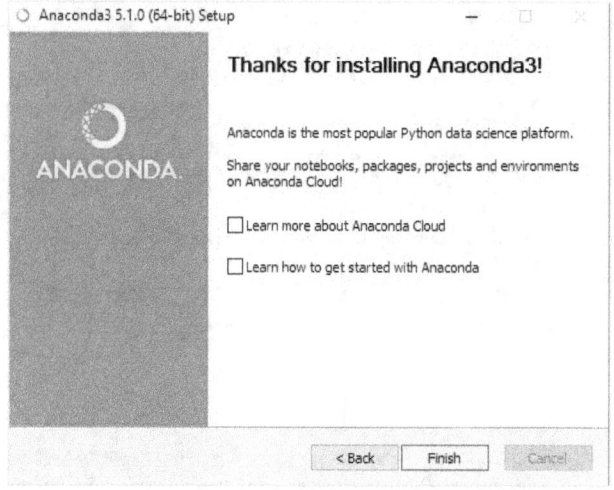

Running your First Program

We have installed environment required to run Python scripts. Now is the time to run our first program. With Anaconda, you have several ways to do so. We will see two of those in this section.

Go to your window search box and type "Anaconda Navigator" and then select the "Anaconda Navigator" application as shown below:

Anaconda Navigator
Desktop app

Folders

anaconda_navigator - in site-packages

anaconda_navigator - in site-packages

anaconda_navigator-1.7.0-py3.6.egg-info -
in site-packages

anaconda_navigator-1.7.0-py3.6.egg-info -
in site-packages

anaconda-navigator-1.7.0-py36_0

Search suggestions

🔎 Anaconda Navigator - See web results 〉

🔎 anaconda navigator **youtube** 〉

🔎 anaconda navigator **windows** 〉

🔎 anaconda navigator **download** 〉

🔎 anaconda navigator **app** 〉

🔎 Anaconda Navigator

Anaconda Navigator Dashboard will appear that looks like this.

Note: It takes some time for Anaconda Navigator to start, so be patient.

From the dashboard, you can see all of the tools available to develop your python applications. In this book we will mostly use "Jupyter Notebook" (second from top). Though in this chapter we shall also see how to run python script via "Spyder".

Running Scripts via Jupyter Notebook

Jupyter notebook runs in your default browser. From the navigator, launch "Jupyter Notebook" (Second option from the top).

Another way to launch Jupyter is by typing "Jupyter Notebook" in the search box and selecting the "Jupyter Notebook" application from the start menu as shown below:

Jupyter Notebook
Desktop app

Folders

🗋 **jupyter_notebook_**config.d - in jupyter

🗋 **jupyter_notebook_**config.d - in jupyter

Documents

🗋 **jupyter-notebook-**script

🗋 **jupyter_notebook_**config

Search suggestions

🔎 jupyter notebook - See web results ⟩

🔎 jupyter notebook **download** ⟩

🔎 jupyter notebook **login** ⟩

🔎 jupyter notebook **online** ⟩

🔎 jupyter notebook **app** ⟩

🔎 jupyter notebook **images** ⟩

🔎 jupyter notebook

Jupyter notebook will launch in a new tab of your default browser.

To create a new notebook, click "new" button at the top-right corner of the Jupyter notebook dashboard. From dropdown, select "Python 3."

You will see new Python 3 notebook that looks like this:

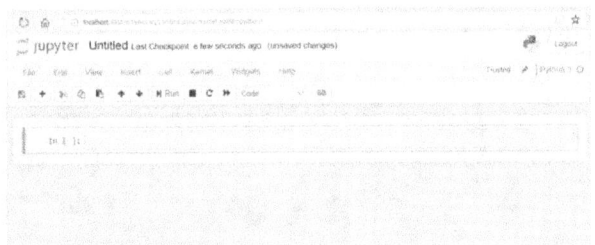

Jupyter notebook consists of cells. Python script is written inside these cells. Let's print hello world using Jupyter notebook. In the first cell of the notebook enter "print('hello world') and press CTRL+ ENTER. The script in the first cell will be executed as shown below:

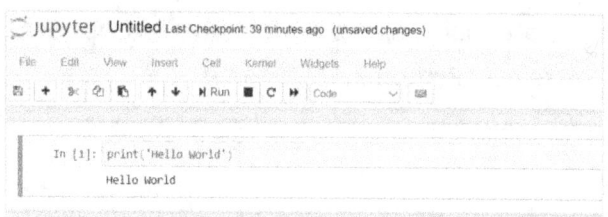

The "print" function prints the string passed to it as parameter, in the output. To create a new cell, click the "+" button from the top left menu as shown below:

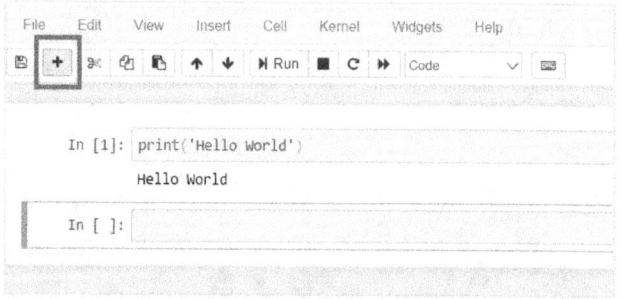

You can write Python script in the new cell and press CTRL + ENTER to execute it.

Running Scripts via Spyder

While Jupyter notebook is a good place to start writing Python programs, once you get comfortable with Python, you should move to Spyder IDE. Spyder allows us to directly create Python files. Spyder is similar to more conventional text editors with options to Run file, Run piece of code, debug code etc.

Just like Jupyter notebook, you can run Spyder from Anaconda Navigator or directly from Start Menu. You will be presented with the following interface once you run Spyder.

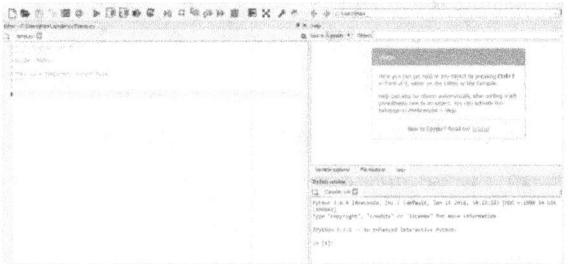

On the left side of the Spyder interface, you can see text editor; this is where you enter your script. On the bottom right you have console window. You can directly execute scripts in the console window. Furthermore, the output of the code written in the editor also appears in the console window. Let's write hello world program in Spyder.

To run script in Python you have two options. You can either click the green triangle from the top menu or you can select the piece of code you want to execute and press CTRL + ENTER from the keyboard. You will see the output in the console window.

What's next?

In this chapter we saw the process of setting up the environment required to run python programs. We wrote our first python program in two different editors. In the next chapter we will start our discussion about Python syntax. Happy Coding!!!

Chapter 3

Python Syntax

To write python code, you need to follow some rules. In programming terms, these rules are collectively called syntax. Python's unique syntax is one of the reasons that novice programmers find it easy to learn and program. In this chapter we shall study python syntax in detail.

Simple Statements

Unlike most of the other object oriented programming languages, Python doesn't require a semi colon at the end of the statement if there is only single statement in the line. In case if you want to write multiple python statements on one line

(Which is highly not recommended), you have to separate them with semi-colon. Take a look at the following example.

Here we write two Python statements on two separate lines. We don't need semicolon.

```
print ("Welcome to Python")
print ("It is fun learning Python")
```

When you execute the above statement, you will see following output:

```
Welcome to Python
It is fun learning Python
```

Now let's write two statements on one line separated by semi colon:

```
print ("Welcome to Python") ;
print ("It is fun learning Python")
```

The output of the above script will be same since they actually are two statements even if they are written on one line.

You can also write a python statement that spans multiple lines. To do so, you have to append backward slash at the end of the line. Backward slash denotes that the statement continues to the next line. Take a look at the following script:

```
sum = 10 + 20 + \
      30 + 40 + \
      50

print(sum)
```

Code Blocks and Indentation

Indentation is one of the most striking features of Python syntax. In almost all of the other programming languages, braces are used to specify the scope of the code block. In Python, indentations specify the scope of the code block. Look at the following code snippet.

```
if 10 > 3:
```

```
    print("This is inside if
block")
    print("This      is      also
inside if block")


print("This      is      outside      if
block")


if 10 < 3:
    print("This is inside if
block")
    print("This      is      also
inside if block")
```

In the script above, the 'if' block evaluates if 10 is greater than 3, and then executes next two print statements that are indented 4 tabs to the right (which is standard). The statements indented are part of the "if block". After that, statement outside the 'if' block executes. The second if block evaluates if 10 is less than 3, which returns false. Therefore the statements that are part of the second 'if' block, indented to the right, do not execute.

Another important point to note is that the 'if' condition is also not enclosed inside braces like other programming languages. The 'if' block starts with a colon, followed by statements indented to the right.

It is pertinent to mention here that all the statements within a code block should have same indentation or else Python will throw an error. Take a look at the following example.

```python
if 10 > 3:
    print("This is inside if
block")
     print("This              has
different indentation")

print("This is outside if
block")
```

If you try to run the above script, you will get an error that looks like this:

```
    File "<ipython-input-4-288993e82763>", line 3
      print("This has different indentation")
      ^
IndentationError: unexpected indent
```

There are several advantages of using indentation for code blocks rather than braces. Indentation forces developers to write readable code with fewer inconsistencies.

Python Identifiers

An Identifier in programming is a name assigned to any variable, function, module or a class. A Python identifier can contains letters from A-Z a-z, numbers from 0-9 and underscore. A python identifier name must begin with a letter or an underscore. Python is a case sensitive language which means "Customer" and "customer" are considered two different identifiers in Python.

Naming Conventions

Here are some python naming conventions:

- Package and module names are all lower case
- Classes are declared in bumpy case with first letter of the individual words capitalized. For instance "CustomerProductRecord" is a valid class name.
- For methods and functions convention is to use lowercase letters with individual words separated by underscores. For example person_name, get_age etc.
- Private variable names begin with single underscore
- Strongly private variable names begin with double underscore

Python Keywords

Keywords are special words that are reserved by python to perform special tasks. For example keyword class is used to define a class. Similarly keyword "for" is used to define a loop. *Keywords cannot be used as identifier or constant names.* Python has following set of keywords.

and	exec	not
assert	finally	or
break	For	Pass
class	From	Print
continue	global	Raise
def	If	Return
del	import	Try
elif	In	While
else	Is	With
except	lambda	Yield

Capturing User Input

Capturing user input is one of the most fundamental programming tasks. Python makes it simple. In Python 3, you can use the input() function and pass it the string that you want to display to the user. Take a look at the following screen shot:

```
text = input("Please enter your name!")
Please enter your name!
```

Anything you enter in the textbox will be stored inside the text variable.

What's next?

This chapter presented brief overview of Python syntax. The rest of the book follows the conventions and syntax described in this chapter. In the next chapter, we will study basic Python data types. We shall see what different types of data python can hold and how to declare variables to store the data. Happy Coding!!!

Chapter 4

Variables and Data Types

A software application consists of two fundamental parts: Logic and Data. Logic consists of the functionalities that are applied on data to accomplish a particular task. Application data can be stored in memory or hard disk. Files and databases are used to store data on hard disk. In memory, data is stored in the form of variables.

Definition of Variable

Variable in programming is a memory location used to store some value. Whenever you store a value in a variable, that value is actually being stored at physical location in memory. Variables can be thought of as reference to physical memory location. The size of the memory reserved for a variable depends upon the type of value stored in the variable.

Creating a Variable

It is very easy to create a variable in Python. The assignment operator "=" is used for this purpose. The value to the left of the assignment operator is the variable identifier or name of the variable. The value to the right of the operator is the value assigned to the variable. Take a look at the following code snippet.

```
Name  = 'Mike'           # A
string variable
Age   = 15               # An
integer variable
Score = 102.5            # A
floating type variable
Pass  = True             # A
boolean Variable
```

In the script above we created four different types of variables. You can see that we did not specify the type of variable with the variable name. For instance we did not write "string Name" or "int Age". We only wrote the variable name. This is because Python is a loosely typed language. Depending upon the value being stored in a variable, Python assigns type to the variable at runtime. For instance when Python interpreter interprets the line "Age = 15", it checks the type of the value which is integer in this case. Hence, Python understands that Age is an integer type variable.

To check type of a variable, pass the variable name to "type" function as shown below:

```
type(Age)
```

You will see that the above script, when run, prints "int" in the output which is basically the type of Age variable.

Python allows multiple assignment which means that you can assign one value to multiple variables at the same time. Take a look at the following script:

```
Age = Number = Point = 20
#Multiple Assignment

print (Age)
print (Number)
print (Point)
```

In the script above, integer 20 is assigned to three variables: Age, Number and Point. If you print the value of these three variables, you will see 20 thrice in the output.

Python Data Types

A programming application needs to store variety of data. Consider scenario of a banking application that needs to store customer information. For instance, a person's name and mobile number; whether he is a defaulter or not; collection of items that he/she has loaned and so on. To store such variety of information, different data types are required. While you can create custom data types in the form of classes, Python provides six standard data types out of the box. They are:

- Strings
- Numbers
- Booleans
- Lists
- Tuples
- Dictionaries

Strings

Python treats string as sequence of characters. To create strings in Python, you can use single as well as double quotes. Take a look at the following script:

```
first_name = 'mike' # String
with single quotation
last_name = " johns" # String
with double quotation
full_name   =   first_name   +
last_name        #        string
concatenation using +
print(full_name)
```

In the above script we created three string variables: first_name, last_name and full_name. String with single quotes is used to initialize the variable "first_name" while string with double quotes initializes the variable "last_name". The variable full_name contains the concatenation of the first_name and last_name variables. Running the above script returns following output:

```
mike johns
```

Numbers

There are four types of numeric data in python:

- int (Stores integer e.g 10)
- float (Stores floating point numbers e.g 2.5)
- long (Stores long integer such as 48646684333)
- complex (Complex number such as 7j+4847k)

To create a numeric Python variable, simply assign a number to variable. In the following script we create four different types of numeric objects and print them on the console.

```
int_num = 10          # integer
float_num = 156.2   #float
long_num             =            -
0.5977485613454646   #long
complex_num       =        -.785+7J
#Complex

print(int_num)
print(float_num)
print(long_num)
print(complex_num)
```

The output of the above script will be as follows:

```
10
156.2
-0.5977485613454646
(-0.785+7j)
```

Boolean

Boolean variables are used to store Boolean values. True and False are the two Boolean values in Python. Take a look at the following example:

```python
defaulter = True
has_car = False

print(defaulter and has_car)
```

In the script above we created two Boolean variables "defaulter" and "has_car" with values True and False respectively. We then print the result of the AND operation on both of these variables. Since the AND operation between True and False returns false, you will see false in the output. We will study more about the logical operators in the next chapter.

Lists

In Python, List data type is used to store collection of values. Lists are similar to arrays in any other programming language.

However Python lists can store values of different types. To create a list opening and closing square brackets are used. Each item in the list is separated from the other with a comma. Take a look at the following example.

```
cars = ['Honda', 'Toyota',
'Audi', 'Ford', 'Suzuki',
'Mercedez']
print(len(cars))        #finds
total items in string
print(cars)
```

In the script above we created a list named cars. The list contains six string values i.e. car names. Next we printed the size of the list using len function. Finally we print the list on console.

The output looks like this:

```
6
['Honda', 'Toyota', 'Audi', 'Ford', 'Suzuki', 'Mercedez']
```

Tuples

Tuples are similar to lists with two major differences. Firstly, opening and closing braces are used to create tuples instead of lists that use square brackets. Secondly, tuple once created is immutable which means that you cannot change tuple values once it is created. The following example clarifies this concept.

```
cars = ['Honda', 'Toyota',
'Audi', 'Ford', 'Suzuki',
'Mercedez']


cars2 = ('Honda', 'Toyota',
'Audi', 'Ford', 'Suzuki',
'Mercedez')


cars [3] = 'WV'


cars2 [3] = 'WV'
```

In the above script we created a list named cars and a tuple named cars2. Both the list and tuple contains list of car names. We then try to update the third index of the list as well as tuple with a new value. The list will be updated but an error will be thrown while trying to update the tuple's third index. This is due to the fact that tuple, once created cannot be modified with new values. The error looks like this:

```
TypeError                           Traceback (most recent call last)
<ipython-input-17-d571617c1fe4> in <module>()
      5 cars [3] = 'WV'
      6
----> 7 cars2 [3] = 'WV'

TypeError: 'tuple' object does not support item assignment
```

Dictionaries

Dictionaries store collection of data in the form of key-value pairs. Each key-value pair is separated from the other via comma. Keys and values are separated from each other via colon. Dictionary items can be accessed via index as well as keys. To create dictionaries you need to add key-value pairs inside opening and closing parenthesis. Take a look at the following example.

```
cars        =        {'Name':'Audi',
'Model':                    2008,
'Color':'Black'}


print(cars['Color'])
```

```
print(cars.keys())
print(cars.values())
```

In the above script we created a dictionary named cars. The dictionary contains three key-value pairs i.e. 3 items. To access value, we can pass key to the brackets that follow dictionary name. Similarly we can use keys() and values() methods to retrieve all the keys and values from a dictionary, respectively. The output of the script above looks like this:

```
Black
dict_keys(['Name', 'Model', 'Color'])
dict_values(['Audi', 2008, 'Black'])
```

What's next?

This chapter briefly sheds light on variables and data types in Python. In the next chapter we will start our discussion about Python operators. Happy Coding!

Chapter 5

Operators

Operators in programming are literals used to perform specific logical, relational or mathematical operations on the operands. Python operators can be divided into following five categories:

- Arithmetic
- Logical
- Comparison
- Assignment
- Membership operators

In this chapter we will discuss these operators with the help of examples.

Arithmetic Operators

Arithmetic operators, as the name suggests, are used to perform arithmetic operations on the operands.

Suppose N1 = 10 and N2 = 5; take a look at the following table to understand arithmetic operators.

Operator Name	Symbol	Functionality	Example
Addition	+	Adds the operands on either side	N1 + N2 = 15
Subtraction	-	Subtracts the operands on either side	N1 − N2 = 5
Multiplication	*	Multiplies the operands on either side	N1 * N2 = 50
Division	/	Divides the operand on left by the one on right	N1 / N2 = 2
Modulus	%	Divides the operand on left by the one on right and returns remainder	N1 / N2 = 0
Exponent	**	Takes exponent of the operand on the left to the power of right	N1 ** N2 = 100000

Take a look at the following example to see arithmetic operators in action:

```
N1 = 10
N2 = 5

print(N1 + N2)
print(N1 - N2)
print(N1 * N2)
print(N1 / N2)
print(N1 ** N2)
```

The output of the script above looks like this:

```
15
5
50
2.0
100000
```

Logical Operators

Logical operators are used to perform logical functions such as AND, OR and NOT on the operands. The following table contains Python logical operators along with their description and functionality. Suppose N1 is True and N2 is false.

Operator	Symbol	Functionality	Example
Logical AND	and	If both the operands are true then condition becomes true.	(N1 and N2) = False
Logical OR	or	If any of the two operands are true then condition becomes true.	(N1 or N2) = True
Logical NOT	not	Used to reverse the logical state of its operand.	not(N1 and N2) =True

Take a look at the following example to see logical operators in action:

```
N1 = True
N2 = False


print(N1 and N2)
```

```
print(N1 or N2)
print(not(N1 and N2))
```

The output of the above script looks like this:

```
False
True
True
```

Comparison Operators

Comparison operators are used to compare the values contained by the operands and returns true or false depending upon the relationship between the operands. Comparison operators are also commonly known as relational operators. Suppose N1 is equal to 10 and N2 is equal to 5, take a look a look at the following table to understand comparison operators.

Operator	Symbol	Description	Example
Equality	==	Returns true if values of both the operands are equal	(N1 == N2) = false

Inequality	!=	Returns true if values of both the operands are not equal	(N1 != N2) = true
Greater than	>	Returns true if value of the left operand is greater than the right one	(N1 > N2) = true
Smaller than	<	Returns true if value of the left operand is smaller than the right one	(N1 < N2) = false
Greater than or equal to	>=	Returns true if value of the left operand is greater than or equal to the right one	(N1 > =N2) = true
Smaller than or equal to	<=	Returns true if value of the left operand is smaller than or equal to the right one	(N1 <= N2) = false

Take a look at the following example to see comparison operators in action:

```
N1 = 10
N2 = 5
```

```
print(N1 == N2)
print(N1 != N2)
print(N1 > N2)
print(N1 < N2)
print(N1 >= N2)
print(N1 <= N2)
```

The output of the script above looks like this:

```
False
True
True
False
True
False
```

Assignment Operators

Assignment operators are used to assign values to the operand. The table below contains information about Python assignment operators. Suppose N1 is equal to 10 and N2 is equal to 5.

Operator	Symbol	Description	Example

Assignment	=	Used to assign value of the right operand to the right.	R = N1 + N2 assigns 15 to R
Add and assign	+=	Adds the operands on either side and assigns the result to the left operand	N1 += N2 assigns 15 to N1
Subtract and assign	-=	Subtracts the operands on either side and assigns the result to the left operand	N1 -= N2 assigns 5 to N1
Multiply and Assign	*=	Multiplies the operands on either side and assigns the result to the left operand	N1 *= N2 assigns 50 to N1
Divide and Assign	/=	Divides the operands on the left by the right and assigns the result to the left operand	N1 *= N2 assigns 2 to N1
Take modulus	%=	Divides the operands on	N1 %= N2 assigns 0

and assign		the left by the right and assigns the remainder to the left operand	to N1
Take exponent and assign	**=	Takes exponent of the operand on the left to the power of right and assign the remainder to the left operand	N1 **= N2 assigns 100000 to N1

Take a look at the following example to see assignment operators in action:

```
N1 = 10; N2 = 5


R = N1 + N2
print(R)


N1 = 10; N2 = 5
N1 += N2
print(N1)
```

```
N1 = 10; N2 = 5
N1 -= N2
print(N1)


N1 = 10; N2 = 5
N1 *= N2
print(N1)


N1 = 10; N2 = 5
N1 /= N2
print(N1)


N1 = 10; N2 = 5
N1 %= N2
print(N1)


N1 = 10; N2 = 5
N1 **= N2
print(N1)
```

The output of the script above looks like this:

```
15
15
5
50
2.0
0
100000
```

Membership Operators

Membership operators are used to check whether the value stored in the operand exists in a particular sequence or not. There are two types of membership operators in Python: 'in' and 'not in'. The in operator returns true if a value is found in a particular sequence. The "not in" operator returns true in the reverse case. Take a look at the following example to see membership operators in action.

```
cars   =   ['Honda',    'Toyota',
'Audi', 'Ford', 'Camery']
print('Honda'  in  cars)    #
Returns True
print('BMW'   in   cars)    #
Returns False
print('Honda' not in cars) #
Returns False
print('BMW'  not  in  cars) #
Returns True
```

The script above returns following output:

```
True
False
False
True
```

What's Next?

In this chapter, we studied basic Python operators with the help of different examples. In the next chapter we will start our discussion about conditional statements. We will study what different types of conditional statements are supported by Python and how they work. Happy Coding!!!

Chapter 6

Conditional Statements

Conditional statements in programming are used to control the flow of a program. Take example of the login page of a website. It asks user to enter username and password. If the username and password are valid, user is granted access to his personal account, otherwise a message is displayed informing the user that username or password is not correct. Here behind the scene conditional statements are being used to check if the password is correct and depending the validation of password, user is either granted access to his personal account or prompted to enter his username and password again. In short, conditional statements are controlling the flow of the application.

There are three main types of conditional statements in Python:

- If
- else
- elif

The "if" statement

The "if" statement is used to evaluate a block of code if the expression that follows it, evaluates to true. This statement may sound complex at the moment but will make sense once you see working example of the "if" statement. Take a look:

```
num1 = 10
```

```
num2 = 20

if num2 > num1:
    print("num2    is    greater
than num1")
```

In the script above we create two variables num1 and num2 with values 10 and 20 respectively. Next, we write an "if" statement that evaluates if num2 is greater than num1, which returns true. Hence the statement that prints "num1 is greater than num2" executes. The output looks like this:

```
num2 is greater than num1
```

Now let's evaluate if num2 is smaller than num1. Execute the following script:

```
num1 = 10
num2 = 20

if num2 < num1:
    print("num2    is    smaller
than num1")
```

Since num2 is not smaller than num1, therefore the "if" block will not execute and you will see nothing in the output.

Conjugating two or more conditions

You can also conjugate two or more than two expressions using logical "OR" and "AND" operators. Take a look at the following script:

```
num1 = 10
num2 = 20
num3 = 30


if num2 < num1 or num3 > num2
:
    print("num2   is   smaller
than num1 OR num3 is greater
than num2")
```

In the script above, two conditions are evaluated conjugated using logical OR operator. The first condition checks if num2 is greater than num1, which is not true. The second condition evaluates if num3 is greater than num2, which returns true. Since the conditions are conjugated using an OR operator, the overall result will be true, hence the statements in the "if" block will execute. The output of the script above looks like this:

```
num2 is smaller than num1 OR num3 is greater than num2
```

Nested "if" statements

You can nest "if" statement inside other "if" statements. Take a look at the following example:

```
num1 = 10
num2 = 20
num3 = 30

if num2 > num1:
    if num3 > num2:
        print("num2          is
greater than num1 and num3 is
greater than num2")
```

The output will look like this:

```
num2 is smaller than num1 OR num3 is greater than num2
```

The "else" statement

The "if" block executes only if the condition that follows it, returns true. What if we want to execute an alternate set of statements if the condition returns false? The "else" statement performs exactly this task. Take a look at the following statement:

```
num1 = 10
num2 = 20

if num1 > num2:
    print("num1   is   greater
than num2")
else:
    print("num2   is   greater
than num1")
```

In the script above the "if" condition checks if num1 is greater than num2, which evaluates to false. Hence, the "if" block is not executed. The control shifts to "else" statement and the statement in the else block executes. The output of the script above looks like this:

```
num2 is greater than num1
```

The "elif" statement

You can evaluate multiple conditions using the "elif" statement. This is best explained with the help of an example:

```
num1 = 10
num2 = 20
num3 = 30

if num1 > num2:
    print("num1   is   greater
than num2")
```

```
elif num2 > num3:
    print("num2    is    greater
than num3")
elif num3 > num2:
    print("num3    is    greater
than num1")
else:
    print("None    of    the
conditions are true")
```

In the script above, the "if" statement checks if num1 is greater than num2, which evaluates to false. Hence the control shifts to first "elif" statement. The first "elif" statement checks if num2 is greater than num3, which again evaluates to false. Hence the control shifts to the next "elif" statement which evaluates to true since num3 is actually greater than num2. Hence the code block for the second "elif" statement will be executed. The output of the script above looks like this:

```
num3 is greater than num1
```

If the conditions for the "if" and all the "elif" statements evaluate to false, the code block that follows the else statement executes.

Nested "elif" Statements

Like "if" statement, you can also have nested "elif" statements. Take a look at the following example.

```
num1 = 10
num2 = 20
num3 = 30

if num1 > num2:
    print("num1    is    greater than num2")
elif num2 > num3:
    print("num2    is    greater than num3")
elif num3 > num2:
    if num1 > num3:
        print("num1            is greater than num3")
```

```
    elif num2 > num1:
        print("num2          is
greater than num1 but smaller
than num3")
else:
    print("None     of     the
conditions are true")
```

In the script above, from the first level, the second "elif" statement that checks if num3 is greater than num2 evaluates to true. However, inside this "elif" statement there are further nested "if" and "elif" statements. The inner "if" statement checks if num1 is greater than num3 which returns false. The control shifts to the inner "elif" statement which checks if num2 is greater than num1, which evaluates to true. Hence, the statement followed by the inner "elif" block executes. The output of the above script looks like this:

```
num2 is greater than num1 but smaller than num3
```

What's Next?

In this chapter, we studied different types of conditional statements and how they can be used to control the flow of a program. In the next chapter we will start our discussion about iteration statements. We will see different types of iteration statements along with their usage. Happy Coding!!!

Chapter 7

Iteration Statements (Loops)

Iteration statements are used to repeatedly execute a piece of code for specific number of times or until a certain condition is satisfied. Imagine you have to perform a task as simple as printing a five character string on screen, 100 times. You will have to write 100 lines of code. Or you will have to use copy-paste. Consider a scenario where you have to repeatedly execute a huge chunk of code. In such a case, it is not convenient to copy paste the code for several reasons: firstly it will significantly increase the code size and secondly it will be difficult to maintain such a code leading to errors. Luckily, iteration statements come to our rescue in such scenarios. Iteration statements are also commonly known as loops.

There are two types of iteration statements in Python:

- The "for" loop
- The "while" loop

The "for" loop

The "for" loop is used to iterate over a collection of items e.g. list, tuple, dictionary etc. The syntax of for loop is as follows:

```
for i in [list]:
    statement 1 …
    statement 2 …
```

Here 'i' is any variable to which a value can be assigned. List is the list of the elements that the "for" loop iterates upon. Take a look at the following example to see for loop in action:

```
cars                          =
['Audi','BMW','Toyota','Honda
','Ford']
```

```
for car in cars:
    print(car)
```

In the script above we create a list of car names. We then use "for" loop to iterate over this list. Let's understand how for loop actually executes behind the scene. During the first iteration the first item of the cars list (the item at index 0) which is "Audi" in this case, is assigned to the car variable. The value of the car variable is printed on the screen. During the second iteration, the second list items is stored in the car variable and printed on the screen and so on. The output of the script above looks like this:

```
Audi
BMW
Toyota
Honda
Ford
```

Using Range Function

What if we want to execute a particular statement without having a list? We can use "range" function to do so. Basically range function also returns an iterate-able sequence that the "for" loop can iterate on. For instance if we want to execute a "for" loop 10 times, we can use range function as follows. Take a look at the following example:

```
for i in range(10):
    print(i)
```

The range function returns a sequence with specified number of integers, starting from 0. The output of the above script will be integers from 0 to 9.

Range function can also be used create a sequence of integers between a specific range. For instance if you want to create sequence of integers from 50 to 100, you can do so as follows:

```
for i in range(50,101):
    print(i)
```

Remember that the sequence returned by range function contains the integer including the lower bound but not the upper bound. Therefore the above script will return integer from 50 to 100 but not 101.

Iterating Over a String

For loop can also be used to iterate over a string. This is because string is actually sequence of characters. Have a look at the script below:

```
for c in 'Hello world':
    print(c)
```

The output will look like this:

```
H
e
l
l
o

w
o
r
l
d
```

The "while" loop

Number of times a "for" loop executes is equal to the number of items in the sequence that the loop operates upon. What if we want a loop that terminates when certain condition is satisfied? The "while" loop is the answer; The "while" loop executes, until a certain condition is met. Syntax of "while" loop is as follows:

```
while (expression = true):
    statement1 …
```

```
statement2 ...
```

Basically "while" loop checks whether the expression that follows it, evaluates to true or not. It keeps executing until the expression returns true.

Take a look at the following script to understand "while" loop

```
i = 1
while i < 11:
    print(i)
    i = i+1
```

In the script above we initialize a variable "i" with integer 1. We then create a "while" loop which checks if the value of variable "i" is less than 11. With each iteration, inside the "while" loop we increment the value of "i" by 1. After the loop has executed 10 times, the value of "i" becomes 11. Therefore, the condition "i" is less than 11 returns false, hence "while" loop terminates.

Let's try to print table of 9 using "while" loop. Take a look at the following script:

```
i = 1
while i < 11:
    print('9 x '+ str(i) + '
= ' + str(i * 9))
    i = i+1
```

The output of the script above looks like this:

```
9 x 1 = 9
9 x 2 = 18
9 x 3 = 27
9 x 4 = 36
9 x 5 = 45
9 x 6 = 54
9 x 7 = 63
9 x 8 = 72
9 x 9 = 81
9 x 10 = 90
```

Continue Statement

Continue statement is used to skip the remaining statements in the loop and to shift the control back to the beginning of the loop. Continue statement can be used inside "for" as well as "while" loop.

Take a look at the following example to see continue statement in action.

```
for i in range(1,11):
    if(i%2) != 0:
        continue
    print(i)
```

In the script above we use "for" loop that iterates over sequence of integers from 1 to 10. In each iteration, we check if the integer is even. To do so, we divide the integer by 2 and check if the result is 0. If the integer is even we do print it on the console, else if the integer is not even, we use continue statement to go back to the beginning of the for loop body, skipping the print statement. The output of the script contains even numbers between 2 and 10 as shown below:

```
2
4
6
8
10
```

Break Statement

Break statement is used to terminate the execution of a loop. Break statement can be used inside "for" as well as "while" loops. Take a look at the following statement to see break statement in action.

```
for i in range(1,11):
    if(i > 5):
        break
    print(i)
```

In the script above, the "for" loop is terminated using break statement when the value of "i" becomes greater than 5.

What's Next?

We have covered most of the fundamental Python concepts. From the next chapter onwards we will divert our attention towards in-depth analysis of advanced Python concepts. In the next chapter we will study Python sequences in detail. We will have an in-depth analysis of lists, tuples and dictionaries and the functions that can be performed on these sequences. Happy Coding!!!

Chapter 8

Lists, Tuples and Dictionaries

We briefly reviewed lists, tuples and dictionaries in *Chapter 4: Variables and Data Types*. They are some of the most important data structures in Python. In this chapter we will see lists, tuples and dictionaries in detail. We will see how they work what are some of the different types of functions associated with them.

Lists

A list in Python is similar to an array in other programming languages. A list stores collection of objects of different types and is mutable.

Creating a List

There are different ways to create a list. The simplest way to create a list is by enclosing comma separated list of items within square brackets and assigning it to a variable as shown in the example below:

```
colors = ['Red', 'Green', 'Blue', 'Yellow', 'White']
```

The script above creates a list named colors. Other ways to create a list are by using constructors [] and list(). As shown below.

```
colors2 = []
colors3 = list()
```

The above script creates two empty lists: colors2 and colors3.

To create list of sequence of integers you can use *range* function and convert into list using list function. The range function returns a list of sequence of integers from 0 to 1 less than the value passed to it as parameter as shown below:

```
nums = list(range(10))
nums
```

The list nums contains integers from 0 to 9. To create a list of sequence of integers between a specified range, you can pass two values to range function. The first value specifies the lower bound (included in the resultant sequence) and the second value specifies the upper bound (excluded in the resultant sequence). The following range function returns list of integers from 50 to 100.

```
nums = list(range(50,101))
nums
```

Accessing List Elements

Lists are indexed which means you can use indexes to access list elements. Lists follow zero based indexes. The first element is stored at the 0th index while the last element is stored at K-1 index, where K is the total number of elements in the list.

In the following example we will access the 2nd element of the list colors:

```
colors = ['Red', 'Green', 'Blue', 'Yellow', 'White']
print(colors[1])
```

The above script prints 'Green' to the output console.

Lists are mutable, which means that you can change item value stored at a particular index. Let's change the value stored at third index from 'Blue' to 'Black'.

```
colors = ['Red', 'Green', 'Blue', 'Yellow', 'White']
print(colors)
colors[2] = 'Black'
print(colors)
```

In the script above we print the colors list on the screen before and after setting the value of the item at third index to 'Black'. The output looks like this:

```
['Red', 'Green', 'Blue', 'Yellow', 'White']
['Red', 'Green', 'Black', 'Yellow', 'White']
```

You can also access multiple list elements at one time using slice operator i.e. colon (:). For instance if you want to access the first three elements of a list, you can use slice operator as follows:

```
colors = ['Red', 'Green',
'Blue', 'Yellow', 'White']
sublist = colors[:3]
print(sublist)
```

The above script returns following result:

```
['Red', 'Green', 'Blue']
```

Similarly, if you want to access the last three elements of a list, execute the following script:

```
colors = ['Red', 'Green',
'Blue', 'Yellow', 'White']
sublist = colors[-3:]
print(sublist)
```

The result looks like this:

```
['Blue', 'Yellow', 'White']
```

Finally, you can also access range of items from a list using slice operator.

```
colors = ['Red', 'Green',
'Blue', 'Yellow', 'White']
sublist = colors[2:4]
```

```
print(sublist)
```

The above function returns range of elements from the 2nd index up to one less than the 4th index i.e. elements at index 2 and 3. The output looks like this:

```
['Blue', 'Yellow']
```

Appending elements to a list

The *append* function can be used to append elements to a list. The item to append is passed as parameter to the 'append' function. Take a look at the following example:

```
colors = ['Red', 'Green', 'Blue', 'Yellow', 'White']
print(colors)
colors.append('Orange')
print(colors)
```

In the script above, we create a list, colors with five items. We print the list on console. We then append an item to the list and again print the list on the console. The output looks like this:

```
['Red', 'Green', 'Blue', 'Yellow', 'White']
['Red', 'Green', 'Blue', 'Yellow', 'White', 'Orange']
```

You can see the newly appended item 'Orange' in the output.

Removing Element from a List

The *remove* function is used to remove element from a list. The element to remove is passed as parameter to the method.

```
colors = ['Red', 'Green',
'Blue', 'Yellow', 'White']
print(colors)
colors.remove('Blue')
print(colors)
```

The output of the script above looks like this:

```
['Red', 'Green', 'Blue', 'Yellow', 'White']
['Red', 'Green', 'Yellow', 'White']
```

You can see that the item 'Blue' has been removed from the list. List elements can also be deleted using index numbers.

```
colors = ['Red', 'Green',
'Blue', 'Yellow', 'White']
print(colors)
del colors[2]
print(colors)
```

To delete list element by index you have to use *del* function followed by the name of the list and the index value passed inside square brackets.

Concatenating List

You can concatenate one list with the other using '+' symbol as shown below:

```
nums1 = [2, 4, 6, 8, 10]
nums2 = [1, 3, 5, 7, 9]

result = nums1 + nums2
print(result)
```

The output looks like this:

```
[2, 4, 6, 8, 10, 1, 3, 5, 7, 9]
```

You can see that the second list is concatenated at the end of the first list.

Using in and not in Functions with Lists

The 'in' and 'not in' functions can be used to check whether an element exists in a string or not.

```
colors = ['Red', 'Green',
'Blue', 'Yellow', 'White']
print('Green' in colors)
print('Orange' in colors)
print('Black' not in colors)
print('Blue' not in colors)
```

The in function returns true for 'Green in colors' since the item 'Green' actually exists within the color string. Similarly for 'Blue' not in colors, false will be returned since 'Blue' exists in colors list. The output for the script above looks like this:

```
True
False
True
False
```

Finding length of List

The *len* function can be used to find total number of elements in a list.

```
colors = ['Red', 'Green', 'Blue', 'Yellow', 'White']
print(len(colors))
```

The script above returns 5, since there are five elements in the colors list.

Sorting a List

You can sort and reverse elements of a list. The elements are sorted alphabetically in case of strings and in ascending order in case of numeric values. Take a look at the following example:

```
colors = ['Red', 'Green', 'Blue', 'Yellow', 'White']
```

```
colors.sort()
print(colors)


nums = [12, 4, 66, 35, 7]
nums.sort()
print(nums)
```

To sort the list, **sort** function is called on the list. Remember, sorting is in-place which means that the existing list is changed rather than returning a new list. The output of the script above looks like this:

```
['Blue', 'Green', 'Red', 'White', 'Yellow']
[4, 7, 12, 35, 66]
```

List of Lists (Matrices)

Lists can be nested inside another list, resulting in a matrix. In the following example we nest three lists with four items inside another list resulting in '3 x 4' matrix.

```
colors = [[1,15,20,36],
          [41,20,54,47],
          [74,45,69,47]]
```

List of lists or matrices also follow zero based index. To access first list, you need to pass zero as index to the outer list. Take a look at the following example:

```
colors = [[1,15,20,36],
          [41,20,54,47],
          [74,45,69,47]]
print(colors[0])
```

The above script prints the first list inside the parent list as shown below:

```
[1, 15, 20, 36]
```

To access a particular value in nested list, first you have to specify the index for the nested list and then the index for the particular value inside that list. For instance if you want to access the element at the third index belonging to the list at first index i.e. 47, you can use the following syntax.

```
colors = [[1,15,20,36],
          [41,20,54,47],
```

```
        [74,45,69,47]]
print(type(colors))
num = colors[1][3]
print(num)
```

Tuples

Like lists, tuples are also used to store collection of different types of objects. However, unlike lists, tuples are immutable which means that once created, tuple elements cannot be changed. You cannot update a tuple, cannot delete tuple element and cannot add new elements to a tuple.

Creating a Tuple

To create a tuple, assign a comma separated list of objects, enclosed within a parenthesis to a variable. Take a look at the following script:

```
colors = ('Red', 'Green',
'Blue', 'Yellow', 'White')
type(colors)
```

In the script above we create a tuple named colors with five items. To confirm the type of the colors variable we use **type** function which confirms that the type of the variable colors is actually a tuple.

Accessing Tuple Elements

Tuple elements can be accessed just like lists using indexes. Take a look at the following script:

```
colors = ('Red', 'Green', 'Blue', 'Yellow', 'White')
print(colors[2])
```

The script above prints tuple element at second index which is 'Blue'.

The slice operator works for tuples too. Take a look at the following example:

```
colors = ('Red', 'Green', 'Blue', 'Yellow', 'White')
print(colors[:3]) # Accessing first three elements
```

```
colors  =   ('Red',   'Green',
'Blue', 'Yellow', 'White')
print(colors[-3:])                #
Accessing last three elements


colors  =   ('Red',   'Green',
'Blue', 'Yellow', 'White')
print(colors[1:3])                #
Accessing elements at index 1
and 2
```

The output of the script above looks like this:

```
('Red', 'Green', 'Blue')
('Blue', 'Yellow', 'White')
('Green', 'Blue')
```

Updating a Tuple

We know that tuples are immutable. The elements in a tuple cannot be updated, added or removed. Let's try to modify the tuple element and verify this fact.

108

```
colors = ('Red', 'Green',
'Blue', 'Yellow', 'White')
colors[2] = 'Orange'
```

In the script above, we assign a new value to the 2nd index of the colors tuple. Try to execute the script above. The following error will occur:

```
-------------------------------------------------------------------
TypeError                                 Traceback (most recent call last)
<ipython-input-7-826025ebd4a8> in <module>()
      1 colors = ('Red', 'Green', 'Blue', 'Yellow', 'White')
----> 2 colors[2] = 'Orange'

TypeError: 'tuple' object does not support item assignment
```

The error clearly says that the new elements cannot be assigned to a tuple.

Finding length of a Tuple

Tuple length can be found using *len* function. This is similar to list. Take a look at the following script:

```
colors = ('Red', 'Green',
'Blue', 'Yellow', 'White')
print(len(colors))
```

The script above returns 5 i.e. total number of elements in the colors tuple.

Finding an Element in Tuple with 'in' and 'not in' Functions

The 'in' and 'not in' functions can be used with tuples to find if an element exists within the tuple. Take a look at the following script:

```
colors = ('Red', 'Green',
'Blue', 'Yellow', 'White')
print('Green' in colors)
print('Orange' in colors)
print('Black' not in colors)
print('Blue' not in colors)
```

The output of the script above looks like this:

```
True
False
True
False
```

Tuple Concatenation

Like lists, the addition operator '+' can be used to concatenate two tuples. In fact, this is one of the ways to add an element to a tuple.

```
colors    =    ('Red',    'Green',
'Blue', 'Yellow', 'White')
orange_color = ('Orange',)
newcolors    =    colors    +
orange_color
print(newcolors)
```

In the script above, we create a tuple colors with five elements. We then create another tuple namely orange_color with one string element 'Orange'. Both the tuples are concatenated which returns a new tuple with 6 elements. The resultant tuple is then printed to the output console. This is one of the ways to add a new element to an existing tuple. The output of the script above looks like this:

```
('Red', 'Green', 'Blue', 'Yellow', 'White', 'Orange')
```

Finding Maximum and Minimum Element within a Tuple

The max and min functions are used to find the maximum and minimum values within a tuple. Take a look at the following script:

```
nums = (2, 4, 6, 8, 10)
print(min(nums))      #      prints
maximum value in tuple
print(max(nums))      #      prints
minimum value in tuple
```

The output of the script above looks like this:

```
2
10
```

The min and max functions can also be used with a List.

Converting List to Tuples

You can convert a list into tuple by passing list to the constructor of the tuple. Take a look at the following example:

```
colors  =   ['Red',   'Green',
'Blue', 'Yellow', 'White']
print(type(colors))
```

```
colors_tuple = tuple(colors)
print(colors_tuple)
```

In the script above we create a list named
colors with 5 items. We then check the type
of the colors variable. We then create
another variable colors_tuple. The colors
list is passed to the constructor of the tuple
and the resultant tuple is stored in the
colors_tuple variable. The newly created
colors_tuple is then printed on the console.
The output of the script above looks like
this:

```
<class 'list'>
('Red', 'Green', 'Blue', 'Yellow', 'White')
```

Dictionaries

Dictionaries store collection of items in the
form of key-value pairs. Keys and values are
for each item is separated with a colon ':'.
Each element is separated from the other
by a comma. The comma separated list of
items is enclosed by braces. Dictionaries are
mutable, which means that you can update

or delete an item from a dictionary and can also add new items to a dictionary.

Creating a Dictionary

```
cars      =      {'name':'Honda',
'model':2013,
'color':'Yellow',  'Air bags':
True}
type(cars)
```

In the script above, we create dictionary cars with 4 items. We then used type function to confirm the type of the cars variable which returns 'dict'.

Accessing Dictionary items

Items within a dictionary can be accessed by passing key as index. Take a look at the following example.

```
cars      =      {'name':'Honda',
'model':2013,
'color':'Yellow',  'Air bags':
True}
model = cars['model']
print(model)
```

In the script above the value for the item with key 'model' is being accessed by passing the key as index value. You will see 2013 in the output.

You can also access all the keys and values within a dictionary using **keys** and **values** function as shown below:

```
cars    =    {'name':'Honda',
'model':2013,
'color':'Yellow', 'Air bags':
True}
print(cars.keys())           #
Accessing      keys      from
dictionary
print(cars.values())         #
Accessing     values     from
dictionary
```

The output of the script above looks like this:

```
dict_keys(['name', 'model', 'color', 'Air bags'])
dict_values(['Honda', 2013, 'Yellow', True])
```

You can also get items from a dictionary in the form of key-value pairs using **items**

function. Take a look at the following
example:

```
cars       =       {'name':'Honda',
'model':2013,
'color':'Yellow', 'Air bags':
True}
print(cars.items())            #
Accessing       items       from
dictionary
```

The output of the script above looks like
this:

```
dict_items([('name', 'Honda'), ('model', 2013), ('color', 'Yellow'), ('Air bags', True)])
```

**Iterating over Dictionary Items, Keys and
Values**

The 'items', 'keys' and 'values' functions
return sequences that can be iterated using
for loops. Take a look at the following
example:

```
cars       =       {'name':'Honda',
'model':2013,
'color':'Yellow', 'Air bags':
True}
for item in cars.items():
```

```
    print(item)
```

The output of the script above looks like this:

```
('name', 'Honda')
('model', 2013)
('color', 'Yellow')
('Air bags', True)
```

Similarly, keys and values can also be iterated using for loops as shown in the following examples:

```
cars      =      {'name':'Honda',
'model':2013,
'color':'Yellow',  'Air  bags':
True}


for key in cars.keys():
    print(key)
```

Output:

```
name
model
color
Air bags
```

Similarly for values:

```
cars      =      {'name':'Honda',
'model':2013,
'color':'Yellow', 'Air bags':
True}


for value in cars.values():
    print(value)
```

Output:

```
Honda
2013
Yellow
True
```

Adding Item to a dictionary

It is very easy to add a new item to a dictionary. You simply have to pass new key in index and assign it some value. Take a look at the following example:

```
cars      =      {'name':'Honda',
'model':2013,
'color':'Yellow', 'Air bags':
True}
```

```
print(cars)
cars['capacity'] = 500
print(cars)
```

In the script above, we create dictionary cars with four items. The dictionary is then printed on the console. Next, a new item is added to the dictionary. The dictionary is then printed on the console again. You will see that the new dictionary will contain five items. The output of the script above looks like this:

```
{'name': 'Honda', 'model': 2013, 'color': 'Yellow', 'Air bags': True}
{'name': 'Honda', 'model': 2013, 'color': 'Yellow', 'Air bags': True, 'capacity': 500}
```

Updating a Dictionary

To update dictionary, pass the key for which you want to update the value as index and assign it a new value. The following example makes it clearer:

```
cars      =     {'name':'Honda',
'model':2013,
'color':'Yellow', 'Air bags':
True}
print(cars)
```

```
cars['model'] = 2015
print(cars)
```

In the script above the items in the cars dictionary are printed before and after updating the value of the item with key 'model'. In the output you can see old and new value for 'model'. The output looks like this:

```
{'name': 'Honda', 'model': 2013, 'color': 'Yellow', 'Air bags': True}
{'name': 'Honda', 'model': 2015, 'color': 'Yellow', 'Air bags': True}
```

Deleting Dictionary Items

Like lists, the 'del' function can be used to delete items from a list. Have a look at the example below:

```
cars      =      {'name':'Honda',
'model':2013,
'color':'Yellow',  'Air  bags':
True}
print(cars)
del cars['model']
print(cars)
```

To delete an item you use **del** function followed by the name of the dictionary. The

120

key of the item that you want to delete is passed as index to the dictionary name. The script above shows items in the cards dictionary, before and after deleting the item with key 'model'. The output looks like this:

```
{'name': 'Honda', 'model': 2013, 'color': 'Yellow', 'Air bags': True}
{'name': 'Honda', 'color': 'Yellow', 'Air bags': True}
```

You can also delete all the items in a dictionary using *clear* function. The following example shows that:

```
cars      =        {'name':'Honda',
'model':2013,
'color':'Yellow',  'Air  bags':
True}
print(cars)
cars.clear()
print(cars)
```

The output of the script above looks like this:

```
{'name': 'Honda', 'model': 2013, 'color': 'Yellow', 'Air bags': True}
{}
```

Finding Dictionary Length

Like tuples and lists, length of a dictionary can be found using *len* function. Take a look at the following example:

```
cars        =        {'name':'Honda',
'model':2013,
'color':'Yellow',  'Air  bags':
True}
print(len(cars))
```

The script above returns 4 since there are 4 elements in the cars dictionary.

Checking the existence of an Item in Dictionary

To check if an item with certain key exists in a dictionary both *in* and **not in** methods can be used. Take a look at the following script:

```
cars       =        {'name':'Honda',
'model':2013,
'color':'Yellow',  'Air  bags':
True}
print('color' in cars)
print('model' not in cars)
```

In the script above, the 'in' operator will return true since the key 'color' exists in the cars dictionary. However the operator 'not in' will return false since the key 'model' also exist in the cars dictionary. The output of the script above looks like this:

```
True
False
```

Copying Dictionaries

To copy one dictionary to the other, you can use *copy* function. Take a look at the following example:

```
cars     =     {'name':'Honda',
'model':2013,
'color':'Yellow', 'Air bags':
True}
cars2 = cars.copy()
print(cars2)
```

In the script above, we create dictionary cars with four items. We then copy this dictionary to another dictionary cars2. The newly created dictionary is then copied on the console. The output looks like this:

```
{'name': 'Honda', 'model': 2013, 'color': 'Yellow', 'Air bags': True}
```

What's next?

In this article we studied lists, tuples and dictionaries which are the most commonly used data structures for storing collections in Python. We saw how these collections are created and what are some of the most commonly used functions that can be applied to these collections. In the next chapter we will see different types of exceptions (errors) in python and how to handle these errors. Happy Coding!

Chapter 9

Exception Handling in Python

Errors and exceptions are part and parcel of a computer program in the development phase. The importance of handling exceptions is reflected by the fact that most of the software companies have a dedicated Quality Assurance (QA) department, responsible for ensuring that the final product is error free. In this chapter we will study what different types of python exceptions are, and how to handle these exceptions.

What is an Exception?

Exception is an event that disrupts the program execution. In simple words, when a Python scripts encounters a situation that it cannot deal with, it raises an exception. In Python, exception is raised in the form of object. Whenever an exception occurs, an object is initialized that contains information about the exception. An exception has to be handled in Python, otherwise the program quits executing.

Unlike most of the other programming languages, Python code is not evaluated at runtime since Python is a loosely typed language. The type of the variable is evaluated at runtime. There are both pros and cons of this approach. The major advantage of this approach is that a user doesn't have to specify the type of the variable while writing a code. A major drawback is that it can lead to exceptions at runtime. We will see this with the help of en example in this article, but first let's see how a simple exception is handled in Python

Syntax for Exception Handing

The syntax for exception handling is as follows:

```
Try:
     #the code that can raise
exception
except ExceptionA
     #the code to execute if
ExceptionA occurs
except ExceptionB
     #the code to execute if
ExceptionA occurs
except ExceptionC
     #the code to execute if
ExceptionA occurs
else:
     #Code  to  execute  if
there is no exception
```

The code that you think can raise an exception is surrounded by *try* block followed by one or more *except* blocks depending upon the type of exceptions that you want to handle. If none of the exceptions occur, the *else* block executes.

Handling Single Exception

Example 1

Take a look at a very simple example of exception handling. Let us first write a program without exception handling. Execute the following script:

```
num1 = 10
num2 = 0
result = num1/num2
print(result)
```

In the script above we have two variables num1 and num2. We try to divide num1 by num2 and print the result on the console. However, num2 contains 0. Therefore, the division will not be successful since a number cannot be divided by zero. An error will be thrown that looks like this:

```
------------------------------------------------------------------
ZeroDivisionError                          Traceback (most recent call last)
<ipython-input-14-0e801cc83d6e> in <module>()
      1 num1 = 10
      2 num2 = 0
----> 3 result = num1/num2
      4 print(result)

ZeroDivisionError: division by zero
```

The name of the exception is
"ZeroDivisionError" and it occurs when a
number is divided by zero. Let's see how we
can handle this exception.

Take a look at the following script:

```
try:
    num1 = 10
    num2 = 0
    result = num1/num2
    print(result)
except ZeroDivisionError:
    print ("Sorry, division by
zero not possible")
else:
    print("Program     executed
without an exception")
```

In the script above, the code that throws an exception is enclosed in a try block. In the previous example, the code threw ZeroDivisionError. Therefore, we handle this exception using *except* literal. Inside the *'except'* block the reason for the exception is printed. Finally, we have an else block that executes if the exception doesn't occur. Since we are dividing num1 by zero, the statement in the *'except'* block will execute and the output will look like this:

```
Sorry, divison by zero not possible
```

Now, if you change the value of num2 in code to 2. The exception will not occur and the output will display the code in the else block that looks like this:

```
5.0
Program executed without an exception
```

Hence, handling an exception prevents a program from crashing.

Example2

A program can throw multiple types of exceptions. Take a look at the following example to understand this concept:

```
try:
    result = a/b
    print(result)
except ZeroDivisionError:
    print ("Sorry, division by
zero not possible")
else:
    print("Program      executed
without an exception")
```

In the script above we try to divide 'a' by 'b'. We have handled the ZeroDivisonError exception. Therefore, if b contains 0, the exception will be handled. Else, if no exception occurs the *else* block will execute.

When you run the script above, you will see following exception:

```
------------------------------------------------------------------------
NameError                                   Traceback (most recent call last)
<ipython-input-1-f57c54e1ec6b> in <module>()
      1 try:
----> 2     result = a/b
      3     print(result)
      4 except ZeroDivisionError:
      5     print ("Sorry, divison by zero not possible")

NameError: name 'a' is not defined
```

From the output you can see that the name of the exception is "NameError" and the exception says that the name 'a' is not defined. This means that we are using a variable without first defining it.

To handle this exception, execute the following code:

```
try:
    result = a/b
    print(result)
except NameError:
    print ("Some    variable/s
are not defined")
else:
    print("Program    executed
without an exception")
```

You can see that different types of exceptions are raised due to different reasons. In order to build a robust program, a user should handle all the possible exceptions. A list of different types of Python exceptions is available at the following link:

https://docs.python.org/3/library/exceptions.html

Handling Multiple Exceptions

To handle multiple exceptions, you just have to stack one exception handling block over the other. Take a look at the following exception:

```
try:
    num1 = 10
    num2 = 2
    result = num1/num2
    print(result)
except ZeroDivisionError:
```

```
    print ("Sorry, division by
zero not possible")
except NameError:
    print    ("Some    variable/s
are not defined")
else:
    print("Program    executed
without an exception")
```

In the script above, both the "ZeroDivisionError" and "NameError" exceptions are handled. Therefore, if you set the value of num2 to 0, the "ZeroDivisionError" exception will occur. However if you try to divide the num1 by 'b', the "NameError" exception will occur since the variable "b" is not defined. Finally if none of the exception occurs, the statement in the **else** block will execute.

Another way to handle multiple exceptions is by using Exception object which is base class for all the exceptions. The Exception object can be used to handle all types of exceptions. Take a look at the following example.

```
try:
    num1 = 10
    num2 = 0
    result = num1/num2
    print(result)
except Exception:
    print ("Sorry, program
cannot continue")
else:
    print("Program    executed
without an exception")
```

In the script above, all the different types of exceptions will be handled by code block for Exception object. Therefore, a generic message will be printed to the user. In the script above, the num2 contains zero. Therefore, the "ZeroDivisionError" exception will occur. The result will look like this:

```
Sorry, program cannot continue
```

What's next?

In this chapter we studies how we can handle exceptions in Python. In the next chapter we will see how to perform file handling tasks with Python. Happy Coding!!!

Chapter 10

Python File Handling

File handling refers to performing variety of operations on different types of file. The most common file handling operations are opening a file, reading file contents, creating a file, writing data to a file, appending data to a file etc. Like every other programming language, Python supports almost all the major file handling functions. In this chapter, we will study how file handling can be achieved with Python.

Opening a File

Before you perform any function on a file, you need to open it. To open a file in python the **open** function is used. It takes 3 parameters: The path to the file, the mode in which the file should be opened and the buffer size in number of lines. The third parameter is optional. The **open** function returns file object. The syntax of the **open** function is as follows:

```
file_object = open(file_name, file_mode, buffer_size)
```

Take a look at the following table for different types of modes along with their description:

Mode	Description
R	Opens file for read only
r+	Opens file for reading and writing
Rb	Only Read file in binary
rb+	Opens file to read and write in binary
W	Opens file to write only. Overwrites existing files with same name
Wb	Opens file to write only in binary. Overwrites existing files with

	same name
w+	Opens file for reading and writing
Wb	Opens file to read and write in binary. Overwrites existing files with same name
A	Opens a file for appending content at the end of the file
a+	Opens file for appending as well as reading content
Ab	Opens a file for appending content in binary
ab+	Opens a file for reading and appending content in binary

The file object returned by the **open** method has three main attributes:

1- name: returns the name of the file
2- mode: returns the mode with which the file was opened
3- closed: is the file closed or not

Take a look at the following example:

Note: Before you execute the script above, create a file *test.txt* and place it in the root directory of the D drive.

```
file_object                    =
open("D:/test.txt", "r+")
print(file_object.name)
print(file_object.mode)
print(file_object.closed)
```

In the script above, we open the test.txt file in the read and write mode. Next we print the name and mode of the file on the screen. Finally we print whether the file is closed or not. The output of the script above looks like this:

```
D:/test.txt
r+
False
```

To close an opened file, you can use **close** method. Take a look at the following example:

```
file_object                    =
open("D:/test.txt", "r+")
print(file_object.name)
print(file_object.closed)
```

```
file_object.close()
print(file_object.closed)
```

In the script above, the test.txt file is opened in r+ mode. The name of the file is printed. Next we check if the file is opened using closed attribute, which returns false, since the file is open at the moment. We then close the file using close method. We again check if the file is closed, which returns true since we have closed the file. The output looks like this:

```
D:/test.txt
False
True
```

Writing Data to a File

To write data to a file, the *write* function is used. The content that is to be written to the file is passed as parameter to the write function. Take a look at the following example:

```
file_object                    =
open("D:/test1.txt", "w+")
```

```
file_object .write( "Welcome
to        Python.\nThe        best
programming language!\n");


file_object .close()
```

In the script above, the file test.txt located
at the root directory of D drive is opened.
The file is opened for reading and writing.
Next two lines of text have been passed to
the write function. Finally the file is closed.

If you go to root directory of D drive, you
will see a new file test1.txt with the
following contents:

```
Welcome to Python.
The        best        programming
language!
```

Reading Data from a File

To read data from a file in Python, the *read*
function is used. The number of bytes to read

from a file is passed as a parameter to the read function. Take a look at the following example:

```
file_object                              =
open("D:/test1.txt", "r+")

sen = file_object.read(12)

print("The file reads: "+sen)


file_object .close()
```

The script above reads the first 12 characters from the test1.txt file that we wrote in the last example. The output looks like this:

```
The file reads: Welcome to P
```

To read the complete file, do not pass anything to the read function. The following script reads the complete test1.txt file and prints its content on the console:

```
file_object                              =
open("D:/test1.txt", "r+")

sen = file_object.read()

print(sen)

file_object .close()
```

The output of the script above looks like this:

```
Welcome to Python.
The best programming language!
```

Renaming and Deleting Python Files

You can rename and delete python files using Python **os** module. To rename a file, the **rename** function is used. The old name of the file is passed as first parameter while new name is passed as second parameter. Take a look at the following example:

```
import os
os.rename(    "D:/test1.txt",
"D:/test2.txt" )
```

The above script renames file test1.txt to test2.txt

To delete a file in Python, the **remove** method is used. Take a look at the following example:

```
import os
os.remove("D:/test.txt")
```

The above script deletes the test.txt file located at the root directory of D drive.

File Positioning

To find the current position of the cursor in file, the *tell* function is used. Take a look at the following example:

```
file_object                    =
open("D:/test2.txt", "r+")
print(file_object.tell())
sen = file_object.read(12)
print(sen)
print(file_object.tell())
file_object .close()
```

In the script above, file test2.txt is opened. We then use to check the current position of the file, which returns 0. Next, the first 12 characters of the file are read. Next, the *tell* function is again called to find the current position of the file cursor. This time it will return 12, since the 12 characters have been just read using the read function. The output looks like this:

```
0
Welcome to P
12
```

What's Next?

In this chapter we studied how files are handled in Python. What the different file handling functions are and how to implement them. In the next chapter we will start our discussion about Functions in Python.

Chapter 11

Functions in Python

If a program has a large piece of code that is required to be executed repeatedly, it is better to implement that piece of code as a function and then call it using a loop. Functions foster code reusability, modularity and integrity. Consider a scenario where you have to add two numbers 100 times. Without function you will have assign values to two variables 100 times, perform the addition and print the result on console. If you are asked to perform subtraction, you will again have to change the plus sign into minus 100 times.

In such a scenario, it is more convenient to write a function that accepts two numbers and performs addition between them. The function can then be called inside a loop. Similarly, if you to change addition to subtraction, you will have to do it at one place.

In this article we will see how to declare Python functions, how to call them, how to return values from them and some other operations.

Function Declaration

The syntax to create a function is as follows:

```
def function_name ():
    #code line 1
    #code line 2
    #code line 3
```

The function declaration starts with **def** keyword followed by the name of the function and opening and closing parenthesis. The parentheses are used for passing information to the function.

Let's write a simple function that prints 'Welcome to Python" on screen.

```
def print_welcome():
    print("Welcome          to
Python")
```

The above script creates a function named ***print_welcome*** . Function declaration completes successfully even if the function body contains errors. This is because a function body is actually evaluated when the function is called.

To call a function, simply type the name of the function followed by pair of parenthesis as shown below:

```
Print_welcome()
```

When the above script executes, the print_welcome function executes and prints "Welcome to Python" on the console. The output looks like this:

Parameterized Functions

In the previous example we left the parenthesis that follow the function name, empty. However these opening and closing parenthesis are used to pass parameters to function. Take a look at the following example:

```
def print_name(name):
    print("Person  name  :"  +
name)

print_name("James")
print_name("Sofia")
print_name("Rick")
```

In the script above, we define a function **print_name** which accepts one parameter name and print it inside the function.

In the function call to the print_name function, we pass the value for the name parameter. We call the print_name function thrice with three different values for the parameter. In the output you will see these values as follows:

```
Person name :James
Person name :Sofia
Person name :Rick
```

A function can have as many parameters as you want. However the sequence of parameters in the function definition must match the sequence in the function call. Take a look at the following function. It accepts three parameters: name, age and gender.

```
def print_details(name, age,
gender):
    print("Person name :" +
name)
    print("Person age :" +
str(age))
```

```
    print("Person gender :" +
gender)
    print("--------------------
-")

print_name("James", 20,
"Male")
print_name("Sofia", 30,
"Female")
print_name("Rick", 25,
"Male")
```

In the script above, we create a function **_print_details._** The function accepts three parameters name, age and gender and prints them on the console. The function has been called thrice with different values for name, age and gender parameters. The output of the above script looks like this:

```
Person name :James
Person age :20
Person gender :Male
-------------------
Person name :Sofia
Person age :30
Person gender :Female
-------------------
Person name :Rick
Person age :25
Person gender :Male
-------------------
```

Returning Values from a Function

Just as you can pass information to a function via arguments (parameters, you can also return values from a function. To return value from a function the **return** keyword is used. Take a look at the following example.

```
def add_number(num1, num2):
    result = num1 + num2
    return result
```

```
result = add_number(10,20)
print("sum of 10 and 20 is :"
+ str(result))

result = add_number(5,15)
print("sum of 5 and 15 is :"
+ str(result))
```

In the above script, we create a function *add_number.* The function accepts two arguments, adds them and returns the resultant sum.

We then call the function twice and pass it two different numbers. The result is printed on the console. The output looks like this:

```
sum of 10 and 20 is :30
sum of 5 and 15 is :20
```

Default Arguments

Python functions can have default values for the parameters, called default arguments. If no argument value is passed for that parameter from the function call, the default value is used. Take a look at the following script:

```
def add_number(num1, num2 =
100):
    result = num1 + num2
    return result

result = add_number(20)
print("sum of 100 and 20 is
:" + str(result))

result = add_number(5,15)
print("sum of 5 and 15 is :"
+ str(result))
```

In the script above we create an **add_number** function. The num2 parameter of the function has default argument value of 100.

The add_number function is called twice. In the first call only one argument is passed i.e. 20. This argument is passed for the num1 parameter. No argument is passed

155

for the num2 parameter. Therefore the default argument value of 100 will be used and the returned result will be 120 (100 + 20).

In the second call to the add_number function, arguments for both num1 and num2 parameters have been passed. Therefore the default argument for num2 i.e. 100 will not be used. The result of the script above looks like this:

Passed by Value or By Reference?

Arguments passed to Python functions are by reference. That means that if the function updates the value of an argument, the value is also updated outside the function. This will become clearer with the help of following example:

```
def update_list(newlist):

newlist.append([20,25,30]);
    return
```

```
numlist = [5,10,15];
print ("Values before
function call", numlist)

update_list( numlist );
print ("Values after function
call", numlist)
```

In the script above, we create a function called **_update_list._** The function accepts a list as parameter and appends another list to it as an item.

We create a list named numlist with 3 items. We then print this list on the console. The list is then passed as argument to the update_list function which appends another list to it as an item. We then print the numlist on the console again. The results show that though numlist list being printed outside the update_list function, the numlist contains the list appended by update_list function. This is because the reference of the numlist was passed to the update_list function. And update inside the function also caused update to the actual list. The output looks like this:

```
Values before function call [5, 10, 15]
Values after function call [5, 10, 15, [20, 25, 30]]
```

Anonymous Functions

You can also create anonymous functions in Python using single line statement without *def* keyword. The anonymous functions are created using lambda expressions and cannot contain multiple expressions.

Take a look at the following example to see how anonymous functions work:

```
result = lambda num1, num2,
num3: num1 + num2 + num3;

print ("Sum of three values :
", result( 5, 15, 25 ))
print ("Sum of three values :
", result( 2, 4, 6 ))
```

In the script above we create an anonymous function that adds three numbers. The function is stored in a variable named result. The function can then be called using this variable. In the above script the function has been called twice with three different parameter values for the function call. The output of the script looks like this:

```
Sum of three values :   45
Sum of three values :   12
```

Local vs. Global Variables

Depending upon their scope, there are two types of variables in Python: Local and Global. Scope of a variable refers to the part of code where a variable can be assessed.

A variable declared inside a function is called a local variable. Local variables cannot be accessed outside the function. On the other hand, a global variable is not declared inside the function and can be accessed anywhere within a program. Take a look at the following example to see difference between global and local variable.

```
total_students = 10 # global
variable

def
passed_students(p_students):
    #accessing global
variable total_students
inside function
    failed_students =
total_students - p_students
    #printing local variable
failed_students
    print("Failed Students: "
+ str(failed_students))

# Accessing global variable
outside function
print("Total students" +
str(total_students))
passed_students(6)
```

In the script above, we define a global variable *total_students*. We then define a function *passed_students.* Inside the function we accessed global variable *total_students*. The function also contains local variable *failed_students*.

Outside the function we again access global variable **total_students** and call the **passed_students** function. We will see that the global variable can be successfully accessed within a function and outside the function. The output looks like this:

```
Total students10
Failed Students: 4
```

Now if you try to access the local variable *failed_students* outside the *passed_students* function as follows:

```
print(failed_students)
```

An exception will be thrown:

```
------------------------------------------------------------------------
NameError                                 Traceback (most recent call last)
<ipython-input-19-7c75ab616d4e> in <module>()
     10 print("Total students" + str(total_students))
     11 passed_students(6)
---> 12 print(failed_students)

NameError: name 'failed_students' is not defined
```

The error shows that *"failed_students"*
variable is not defined. In other words, it
cannot be accessed outside the function in
which it was declared.

What's Next?

In this chapter, we completed our
discussion about Python function. We saw
different ways of creating functions with
the help of examples. In the next chapter,
we will start our discussion about object
oriented programming in Python. Happy
Coding!!!

Chapter 12

Object Oriented Programming in Python

Object oriented programming (OOP) is a programming paradigm in which the application is implemented in the form of objects that imitate real world entities. Objects can have attributes, methods and properties. Anything that contains some information and can perform a function is a candidate of being implemented as an object in OOP. Consider a scenario where you have to develop a first person shooter game using object oriented programming. You have to think about the real world objects that have some information and can perform some functionality in the first person shooter game. Shooter himself is an object since shooter has a name, height, weight, nationality etc. and can perform functions like run, sit, stand, crawl etc.

Similarly, gun is also an entity since gun can shoot, load, reload etc. In this chapter, we will start our discussion about object oriented programming in Python.

Classes

A class is a basic building block of object oriented programming. In simple words, a class serves as a blue print for an object. Another analogy between classes and object is that of map and house. You can tell by reading a map that how the house is structured, where the dining room is, how many rooms are there in the house and so on. You can use one map to build several similar houses. Similarly, one class can be used to create several similar objects.

Take a look at the following example to see how we can create a class in Python. Let's create a simple class person:

```
# Creates class Person
class Person:
```

```
#create class attributes
name = "Jospeh"
age = 28
gender = "Male"
role = "Shooter"

#create class methods
def stand(self):
    print            ("Person
standing")

def sit(self):
    print      ("Person      is
sitting")
```

In the script above we create a class Person
with four attributes and three methods. The
attributes are name, age, gender and role
while the methods are **stand** and **sit**. The
class methods are basically functions but
they are defined inside the class body. It is
important to mention that class methods
take self as first parameter by default. The
literal **self** refers to the class that contains
the method.

As discussed earlier, classes are merely blue prints, they are animated via objects. One class can have multiple objects.

Objects

In Python, everything is treated as an object. Python objects can be broadly divided into two categories:

1- Built in Objects
2- Custom Objects

Built in Objects

Built in objects are the objects belonging to primitive data types. For instance, when you assign an integer to a variable, basically an integer object is stored in that variable. Take a look at the following script:

```
#creates    an    integer    type
object age
age = 28

type(age)
```

In the script above we create an integer object and assign it to age variable. We then check the type of age variable which returns int.

Custom Objects

Custom objects are the objects that implement custom classes. In the previous section we created a class Person. Let's create object of the Person class. Take a look at the following script:

```
person1 = Person()
```

To create custom object, you simply have to write the name of the class followed by a pair of parenthesis and assign it to a named entity (variable) which is *person1* in the above example. Now the object *person1* can be used to access the Person class attributes and methods.

To access class attributes or methods, you can use the object name followed by the dot operator and the name of the attribute or the method. Take a look at the following example:

```
#accessing attributes
f_name = person1.name
print(f_name)
#assessing methods
person1.stand()
```

In the script above, the name attribute of the Person class is accessed via person1 object and the assigned to the f_name variable. The f_name variable is then printed on the screen.

Similarly, the stand function is accessed which prints the statement "Person standing" on the console. The output of the script above looks like this:

```
Jospeh
Person standing
```

Constructor

"Constructor" is a method that executes when a class is instantiated. The processes of creating object of a class is also known as instantiation. To create a constructor in

Python, the __*init*__ method is used. Take a look at the following example to see constructor in action.

```
# Creates class Person
class Person:

    #create constructor
    def __init__(self):
        print("Class     object
created")

    #create class methods
    def stand(self):
        print               ("Person
standing")
```

In the script above, we again create class Person. But this time the class has a constructor which simply prints some text on the screen. The class also contains *stand* method.

Now, when you create the object of the Person class, the constructor will execute and you will see "Class object created" on the console screen. Execute the following script:

```
person1 = Person()
```

The output will be:

```
Class object created
```

Attributes

We know that a value assigned to named entity in Python is actually an object. By the same analogy, the attributes declared inside a class are also objects. This means that objects can contain nested objects. Let's create a primitive string type object and check what attributes the object contains. Take a look at the following script:

```
#Creates   a   string   object
message

message = "I love Python"

#find   all   attributes   of
message object

print(dir(message))
```

In the script above we create a string object named "message". To find all the attributes of an object the *dir* method is used. The output of the above script looks like this:

```
['__add__', '__class__', '__contains__', '__delattr__', '__dir__', '__doc__', '__eq__', '__format__', '__ge__', '__getattribute__', '__getitem__', '__getnewargs__', '__gt__', '__hash__', '__init__', '__init_subclass__', '__iter__', '__le__', '__len__', '__lt__', '__mod__', '__mul__', '__ne__', '__new__', '__reduce__', '__reduce_ex__', '__repr__', '__rmod__', '__rmul__', '__setattr__', '__sizeof__', '__str__', '__subclasshook__', 'capitalize', 'casefold', 'center', 'count', 'encode', 'endswith', 'expandtabs', 'find', 'format', 'format_map', 'index', 'isalnum', 'isalpha', 'isdecimal', 'isdigit', 'isidentifier', 'islower', 'isnumeric', 'isprintable', 'isspace', 'istitle', 'isupper', 'join', 'ljust', 'lower', 'lstrip', 'maketrans', 'partition', 'replace', 'rfind', 'rindex', 'rjust', 'rpartition', 'rsplit', 'rstrip', 'split', 'splitlines', 'startswith', 'strip', 'swapcase', 'title', 'translate', 'upper', 'zfill']
```

Class Attributes vs. Instance Attributes

Python classes have two types of attributes: Class attributes and Instance attributes. The instance attributes are specific to the individual objects of a class and are not shared between the objects. On the other hand, class attributes are shared among all the instances (objects) of a class.

The instance attributes are defined inside a method while the class attributes are defined outside the method. Take a look at the following example to see difference between class and instance attributes.

```python
# Creates class Person
class Person:

#Creates class attribute
    person_count = 0

#Creates method with instance attributes
    def     set_details(self,
name, age, gender):
        #initialize    instance
variables
        self.name = name
        self.age = name
        self.gender = name
        #increment      class
variables
        Person.person_count
+= 1
        print("Details      for
person " +self.name + " have
been stored")
```

In the script above, as usual we create Person class. The class contains one class attribute person_count and a method *set_details*. Inside the *set_details* method, three instance attributes are initialized with the values passed as arguments to the *set_details* method. Inside the method, the person_count attribute is incremented by one. Another difference you can see here is that inside a class, the class attribute is accessed via class name whereas the instance attributes are accessed via keyword *self*.

Let's create an object of Person class and call the *set_details* method on the object.

```
person1 = Person()
person1.set_details("John",
24, "Male")
print("Person     count    "     +
str(person1.person_count))
```

In the script above, we create person1 object of Person class. We then call the *set_details* method using the object and pass some arguments to the method. The method prints the name of the person on console. We then print the class attribute person_count on the screen which will display 1. The output of the script above looks like this:

```
Details for person John have been stored
Person count 1
```

Now, let's create another Person class object.

```
Person2 = Person()
Person2.set_details("Suzi", 31, "Female")
print("Person    count    " + str(person2.person_count))
```

In the script above, we create person2 object of the Person class. This time, the shared attribute person_count will be incremented to 2 since it previously was 1.

The output of the script above looks like this:

```
Details for person Suzi have been stored
Person count 2
```

From the output you can see class attribute person_count is being shared between the two instances person1 and person2 while the instance attribute "name" is not being shared.

Properties

Encapsulation is one of the major building blocks of OOP. Encapsulation refers to providing controlled access to internal class data. The access is controlled via special methods. The special methods are bundled with the class attributes via properties and descriptors.

Why we need Properties?

In this section we will study properties. But first, let's see why we need properties.

Let's create a class named Medicine with three attributes: name, expiration_year and expiration_month. Execute the following script:

```
# Creates class Medicine
```

```python
class Medicine:


#Creates        Medicine        class
constructor
    def   __init__(self,   name,
expiry_year, expiry_month):
        #initialize    instance
variables

        self.name = name
        self.expiry_year       =
expiry_year
        self.expiry_month      =
expiry_month

    def getExpiryDate(self):
        print               ('The
expiration     date     is     :
'+str(self.expiry_month)+'/'+
str(self.expiry_year))
```

Now let's create an object of the Medicine
class.

```
medicine1  =  Medicine("xyz",
2020, 15)
```

In the script above, the constructor of the Medicine class assigns 15 as the month number to the expiry_month. To see the expiry date, call the ***getExpiryDate*** method using the medicine1 object as shown below:

```
medicine1.getExpiryDate()
```

Technically, any number can be assigned to the month. However, logically there are only 12 months in a year. So the number should be between 1 and 12. This is where properties come handy. Using properties you can control the value assigned and retrieved from the class members.

Take a look at the following script to see how properties can be created:

```
# Creates class Medicine
class Medicine:


#Creates     Medicine     class
constructor
```

```python
    def __init__(self, name,
expiry_year, expiry_month):
        #initialize    instance
variables

        self.name = name
        self.expiry_year    =
expiry_year
        self.expiry_month    =
expiry_month


    #Creates        expiry_month
property
    @property
    def expiry_month(self):
        return
self.__expiry_month


    #Create property setter
    @expiry_month.setter
    def     expiry_month(self,
expiry_month):
        if expiry_month < 1:
```

```python
        self.__expiry_month = 1
        elif expiry_month > 12:

        self.__expiry_month = 12
        else:

        self.__expiry_month = expiry_month

    def getExpiryDate(self):
        print('The expiration date is : '+str(self.expiry_month)+'/'+str(self.expiry_year))
```

To create a property for an attribute, you have to create method with the same name as the name of the attribute. For instance in the above script we wanted to create "expiry_month" property, therefore we created a method "expiry_month" and inside the method we return the value for "expiry_month" attribute using self and double underscore syntax. Remember that the property method must be decorated with the **@property** literal as shown in the script above.

Once the property is created, the next step is to set the rules on the property. Property setter is used for this purpose. The following script sets the rule on the "expiry_month" property.

```
#Create property setter
   @expiry_month.setter
   def     expiry_month(self,
expiry_month):
       if expiry_month < 1:

self.__expiry_month = 1
       elif  expiry_month  >
12:

self.__expiry_month = 12
       else:

self.__expiry_month       =
expiry_month
```

The logic implemented by the above script is simple. If the value assigned to the expiry_month is less than 1, then assign 1 to the expiry_month attribute. Else if the value assigned is greater than 12, assign 12 to the expiry_month variable. Finally, if the value assigned is between 1 and 12, assign that value.

Execute the following script:

```
medicine1 = Medicine("xyz",
2020, 15)
medicine1.getExpiryDate()
```

In the script above, we create medicine1 object of Medicine class. Using the constructor, 15 is assigned as the value for expiry_month attribute. But since we have an expiry_month property, 12 will be assigned to the expiry_month attribute. If you call the **getExpiryDate** method, you will see 12 as expiry_month as shown in the output below:

```
The expiration date is : 12/2020
```

Static Methods

Class methods are similar to functions with two major differences. Class methods are defined inside class body. Class methods take "self" as the first parameter. In this chapter we have seen several examples of instance methods. Instance methods are the methods that are called via class object. There is another category of methods that can be called using class name. These methods are called static methods. Take a look at the following example to see static methods in action:

```
#Creates Person Class
class Person:


    @staticmethod
    def run():
        print    ("Person    is
running")
```

```
def stand(self):
    print    ("Person    is
standing")
```

In the script above, we create a class Person with one static method *run* and with one non static method *stand*. There are two differences between a static and non-static method in Python. A static method has to be decorated with *@staticmethod* decorator. On the other hand, non-static method doesn't require any decorator. Similarly, a static method doesn't need *self* as first parameter while the non-static method requires *self* as first parameter.

Let's call the static method *run* via Person class.

```
Person.run()
```

The output of the script above looks like this:

```
Person is running
```

Special Methods

Special methods or Magic methods are used to add special functionality to a class. The name of a special method starts and ends with double underscores. The constructor **__init__** is also a type of special methods. Other examples of special methods include str, del etc.

Primitive objects also contain special methods. For instance, **int** object contains **__add__** method which adds two integers. Take a look at the following example:

```
#Adding two numbers
int.__add__(15, 30)
```

The output of the above script will be 45.

The __add__ method

Special methods can be overridden. For instance you can override **__add__** special method to add two or more custom classes. Take a look at the following example to see special Methods in action.

```
# Creates class Person
class Person:
```

```
#Creates method with instance
attributes
    def __init__(self, age):
        #initialize    instance
variables
        self.age = age


#Overriding   __add__   special
method
    def __add__(self, other):
        return   self.age   +
other.age
```

In the script above, we create a class named
Person. The class has one attribute age
which is initialized via constructor. The
__*add*__ method is overridden inside the
Person class to add the age attribute of this
class with the age attribute of the class
object passed to the right side of the "+"
operator.

Now when the two objects of the Person class are added via the "+" operator, actually the values for the age attributes of the objects will be added. Take a look at the following script:

```
person1 = Person(10)
person2 = Person(20)
sum_of_age    =    person1    +
person2
print(sum_of_age)
```

In the script, 30 will be printed on the screen since sum of the age of person1 and person2 objects is 30.

The __gt__ method

The __gt__ special method is used to compare two or more classes for comparison. If the attribute of the class on the rleft hand side of the ">" is greater than the attribute of the class on the right hand side, the __gt__ method returns true, else it returns false. Let's modify our Person class to override the __gt__ method for the

comparison of age attribute. Take a look at
the following script:

```
# Creates class Person
class Person:


#Creates method with instance
attributes
    def __init__(self, age):
        #initialize  instance
variables
        self.age = age


#Overriding __add__ special
method
    def __add__(self, other):
        return  self.age  +
other.age


#Overriding __gt__ special
method
    def __gt__(self, other):
```

```
        return    self.age    >
other.age
```

Now, let's create two objects of Person class again and compare their age using ">" operator. Take a look at the following script:

```
person1 = Person(10)
person2 = Person(20)
person1 > person2
```

The value for person1 age attribute is 10 while the value for person2 age attribute is 20. Next, person1 object is being compared to person2 object using ">" operator. But since person1 object's age attribute is less than person2's age attribute, False will be returned.

The __*str*__ method

The __*str*__ method is called when the object is used as string. For instance when you pass the object to print method, the

188

___*str*___ method of the object executes. Like any other special methods, the ___*str*___ method can also be overridden. Take a look at the following example to see how we can override ___*str*___ method of the Person class so that it prints the name of the Person.

```
# Creates class Person
class Person:


#Creates method with instance
attributes
    def __init__(self, name):
        #initialize instance
variables
        self.name = name


    def __str__(self,):
        return "The person is
" + self.name
```

Let's create object of the Person class and try to print on the console:

```
person1 = Person("James")
print(person1)
```

When the script above is executed, the **_str_** method of the Person class executes which produces following output:

```
The person is James
```

Local vs. Global Variables

Like instance and class attributes, variables in Python also have two types: Global variables and local variables. Any variable defined outside the function body is called global variable while variable defined inside the function body is called local variable. Take a look at the following example to see local and global variables in action:

```
#declare global variable
count = 1;

def print_count():
```

```python
    #Accessing            global
variable
    print("Accessing      global
variable  inside  function  :" +
str(count))
    num = 2;

print(count)
print_count()
print(num)
```

In the script above, we first declare a global variable count. The global variable is then accessed inside the ***print_count*** function. Inside the function a local variable "num' is also declared.

Finally, global variable "count" and local variable "num" are accessed outside the function. You will see that the above code will return an error since "num" is a local variable and cannot be accessed outside the ***print_count*** function. The output of the above script looks like this:

```
-------------------------------------------------------------------------------
NameError                                    Traceback (most recent call last)
<ipython-input-49-2c4ee615bb26> in <module>()
     10  print(count)
     11  increment_count()
---> 12  print(num)

NameError: name 'num' is not defined
```

You can see that since we tried to access
the local variable "num" outside the
function, an error was thrown that "num" is
not defined.

Modifiers

Modifiers in Python are used to specify the
scope of a variable. Like most of the other
programming languages, Python has three
access modifiers: Public, Private and
Protected. Variables with Public access
modifier can be accessed anywhere within
the program. Public variables names do not
have leading underscore before their
names. On the other hand, variables with
private modifiers can only be accessed
within the class. Private variable names
start with double underscore. Finally,
protected variables can be accessed within
the class and within the child classes (We

will see parent child classes in the next chapter).

Take a look at the following example to see Modifiers in action:

```
#Creating Person Class
class Person:

    def __init__(self, name,
age, gender):
        #Private Variable
        self.__age = age
        #Public Variable
        self.name = name
        #Protected Variable
        self._gender = gender
```

In the script above we have a Person class with three instance variables: name, age and gender. The name variable is public; age variable is private while the gender variable is protected.

Let's create an object of the Person class and try to access the variables outside the person class. Take a look at the following script:

```
person1 = Person("John", 20,
"Male")
#accessing public variable
print(person1.name)
#accessing private variable
print(person1.age)
```

In the script above we first access the public variable name via the person1 object of the Person class. We then access the private variable age of the Person class. In the output you will see that we will be able to access the name variable since it is public but an error will be thrown when we try to access private variable age, outside the Person class. The output of the script looks like this:

```
John
-------------------------------------------------------------------
AttributeError                          Traceback (most recent call last)
<ipython-input-58-344f0af8bdac> in <module>()
      3 print(person1.name)
      4 #accessing private variable
----> 5 print(person1.age)

AttributeError: 'Person' object has no attribute 'age'
```

The error says that Person object has no attribute age. This is because age is private and cannot be accessed outside the Person class.

Conclusion & What's Next?

In this chapter we started our discussion about Object Oriented Programming in Python. We saw different OOP concepts including classes, objects, attributes, methods, modifiers etc. In the next chapter we will study what is Inheritance and how it is implemented in Python. Happy Coding!!!

Chapter 13

Inheritance & Polymorphism

In the previous chapter we started our discussion about object programming (OOP) and covered most of the basic OOP concepts. There are three pillars of OOP: data encapsulation, inheritance and polymorphism. In the previous chapter we studied how access modifiers and properties are used to implement data encapsulation in Python. In this chapter we will study inheritance and polymorphism.

Inheritance Basics

Inheritance in programming refers to the ability of a class to inherit methods and attributes of other classes. This is similar to real world inheritance. A child inherits some of the characteristics of her parents; in addition to her own unique characteristics. A class that inherits another class is called child class or derived class and the class that is inherited by another class is called parent or base class.

The child and parent classes have is "IS-A" between them. For instance a child class car is a vehicle which is its parent class. Similarly, employee is a person. As a rule of thumb, if multiple classes have some common methods and attributes, a parent class should be defined that contains those methods and attributes. The parent class can then be inherited by the multiple child classes. This will be clear with the help of an example.

Let's create a simple class named "Parent" with one method. We will also create a class named child that inherits the "Parent" class.

```
#Create Class Parent
class Parent:
    def methodA (self):
        print("Hello, I am a
Parent class method")
```

```
#Create    Class    Child    that
inherits Parent
class Child(Parent):
    def methodB (self):
        print("Hello, I am a
Child class method")

#Create object of class Child
child = Child()
#Access Parent class method
child.methodA()
#Access Child class method
child.methodB()
```

In the script above we create a Parent class and a Child class. The Child class inherits the Parent class. To inherit a class, you just have to pass the parent class name inside the parenthesis that follow the child class name. In the above script Parent class contains a method named **methodA**, while the child class also contains a method named *methodB.* We then create a child class object named "child". From this "child" object we call the *methodA*. You can see that though Child class doesn't contain *methodA*, but since it is inheriting Parent class which contains *methodA*, therefore the Child class object can also access this method. Finally we call the Child class method *methodB.* The output of the script above looks like this:

```
Hello, I am a Parent class method
Hello, I am a Child class method
```

Like methods, the child class also inherits attributes from parent class. Take a look at the following example:

```
#Create Class Parent
class Parent:
    name =""
    age = ""
    def methodA (self):
        print("Hello, I am a
Parent class method")
```

```python
#Create    Class    Child    that
inherits Parent
class Child(Parent):
    def methodB (self):
        print("Hello, I am a
Child class method")


#Create object of class Child
child = Child()
#Access Parent class method
child.methodA()
#Access Child class method
child.methodB()
#Access       parent       class
attributes
child.name = "Jacob"
child.age = 10
print(child.name  +  "  "  +
str(child.age))
```

In the script above, we have a parent class with two attributes name and age, and one method ***methodA***, in child class we access the method and attributes and display their values on the console.

Multiple Child Classes

Multiple child classes can inherit from a parent class. Take a look at the following script:

```
#Create Class Parent
class Parent:
    def methodA (self):
        print("Hello, I am a Parent class method")


#Create Class Child1 that inherits Parent
class Child1(Parent):
    def methodB (self):
        print("Hello, I am a Child1 class method")


#Create Class Child2 that inherits Parent
class Child2(Parent):
```

```python
    def methodC (self):
        print("Hello, I am a
Child2 class method")


#Create      object   of   class
Child1
child1 = Child1()
#Access Parent class method
child1.methodA()
#Access Child1 class method
child1.methodB()


#Create      object   of   class
Child2
child2 = Child2()
#Access Parent class method
child2.methodA()
#Access Child1 class method
child2.methodC()
```

In the script above, we have two child classes Child1 and Child2 that inherit the parent class named Parent. Both the child classes have now access to the Parent class method i.e. **methodA**, the output of the script above looks like this:

```
Hello, I am a Parent class method
Hello, I am a Child1 class method
Hello, I am a Parent class method
Hello, I am a Child2 class method
```

Calling Parent Class Constructor from Child Class

We know that a class inherits parent class and its attributes. But a question arises here that how can we initialize the attributes of the parent class using child class constructors. For instance, if there are two attributes in the parent class and 1 attribute in the child class. How do we initialize these three attributes using child class constructor?

Python provides simple solution to this problem. The arguments for the parent and child class constructors are passed to the child class. Inside the child class constructor, the parent class constructor is called and arguments for the parent class constructor are passed to it. The remaining arguments are used to initialize the child class attributes. Take a look at the following example:

```
#Create Vehicle Class
class Vehicle:
    #Constructor    for    the
Parent class
    def __init__ (self, name,
color):
        self.name = name
        self.color = color


#Create    Bike    Class    that
inherits Vehicle Class
class Bike(Vehicle):
    #Constructor    for    the
child class
    def __init__ (self, name,
color, price):
        #Call    to    Vehicle
class    Constructor    from    Bike
class
```

```
        Vehicle.__init__
(self, name, color)

        self.price = price


#Create Vehicle Class Object

bike                          =
Bike("Honda","Black",25000)

#Access        parent        class
attributes

print(bike.name)

print(bike.color)

#Access child class attribute

print(bike.price)
```

In the script above we create Parent class "Vehicle" with two attributes: name and color. The parent class constructor initializes these two attributes. We then defined a child class "Bike" that inherits class Vehicle. Child class has one attribute i.e. price which is initialized via child Bike class constructor. However the Bike class constructor takes three parameters name, color and age. Inside the Bike class constructor, the Vehicle class constructor is called and the name and color attributes are passed to Vehicle class constructor. While the price argument is used to initialize the child class attribute price.

We create object of the Bike class and pass it values for name, color and price attributes. We then print these values on the console. The output of the above script looks like this:

```
Honda
Black
25000
```

Multiple Inheritance

We know that a parent class can be inherited by multiple child classes. This is the type of inheritance supported by programming languages like Java and C#. However, in Python, one child class can also inherit multiple parent classes. This is called multiple inheritance.

The following example will further clear the concept of multiple inheritance.

```
class Vehicle:
    def      showVehicleDetails
(self):
        print("I    am    vehicle
class")


class Sedan:
    def      showSedanDetails
(self):
        print("I    am    sedan
class")


#Create    Class    Car    that
inherits Vehicle and Sedan
class Car(Vehicle,Sedan):
    def      showCarDetails
(self):
        print("I    am    car
class")


#Create object of car Class
car = Car()
```

```
#Access Vehicle class method
car.showVehicleDetails()
#Access Sedan class method
car.showSedanDetails()
#Access child class method
car.showCarDetails()
```

In the script above we have three classes Vehicle, Sedan and Car. The Car class inherits both Vehicle and Sedan class. We then create the object of the Car class and access the Vehicle and Sedan class methods from the car class object. The example shows that a child class that inherits multiple parents has access to all the attributes and methods of all the parent classes. The output of the above example looks like this:

```
I am vehicle class
I am sedan class
I am car class
```

Method Overriding

In addition to having access to parent class methods, a child class can also override parent class method by providing its own definition for the same method name. Take a look at the following example to understand this concept:

```
#Create Person Class
class Employee:
    def printdetails (self):
        print("I      am      an
employee of this company")


#Create  Class  Manager  that
inherits Employee
class Manager(Employee):
    def printdetails (self):
        print("I  am  a  Manager
of this company")

manager = Manager()
manager.printdetails()
```

In the script above, we created two classes: Employee and Manager. The Employee class contains a method *printdetails.* The Manager class inherits the Employee class which means that the Manager class has access to the *printdetails* method of the Employee class. However in the Manager contains its own definition of the *printdetails* method. Now when you create the object of the Manager class and call the *printdetails* method, the method that is overridden in the child class will be called instead of the parent class method as shown in the following output:

```
I am a Manager of this company
```

Polymorphism

The world polymorphism literally refers to "ability to adopt multiple shapes". In programming, polymorphism refers to the capability of a method to behave differently depending upon different scenarios such as number and type of parameters of a method and the type of object that calls the method(whether it is child or parent class object)

A simple example of polymorphism is the addition operator. When you use addition operator to add two numbers, the addition operator works like mathematical addition operator and returns the sum of the operands. However, if the same addition operator is used to add two string, the resultant value is a concatenated string. Take a look at a simple example:

```
#Using addition operator for sum
x = 10
y = 20


result = x + y
print(result)


#using addition operator for string concatenation


x = "Welcome"
y = "to Python"
```

```
result = x + y
print(result)
```

In the script above we assign two numeric values to variables x and y. We then use addition operator to add these values and store the sum in the result variable. We then print the result variable on screen which is a numeric variable. This shows that addition operator adds two numeric operands. Next, we assign two string type values to x and y variables and again use addition operator. This time the addition operator concatenates two strings. The example shows how addition operator follows polymorphism depending upon the operands.

In custom classes, polymorphism is implemented via method overloading and method overriding. We studied method overriding in the previous section, here we shall see method overloading.

Method overloading refers to the ability of a method to perform different function based on the arguments passed to it. Take a look at a simple example of method overloading:

```
#Create Employee
class Employee:
    def printname (self, name
= None):
        if name == None:
            print("Hello,      I
am an employee")
        else:
            print("Hello,      I
am an employee. My name is
",name)
```

In the script above we create a class Employee with one method **printname**. The **printname** method has one optional parameter i.e. name. The **printname** method can be called with one string type argument or without any argument. If the method is called with no argument, the statement "Hello, I am an employee" will be printed on the console. If the **printname** method is called with a string type argument, the statement "Hello, I am an employee. My name is ",name" will be printed on the screen with the argument replacing the name variable. Let's create an object of Employee class and call the **printname** method with and without any argument.

```
emp = Employee()
emp.printname()
emp.printname("Joseph")
```

The output of the above script looks like this:

```
Hello, I am an employee
Hello, I am an employee. My name is  Joseph
```

Conclusion and What's Next?

In this chapter we studied two of the most important OOP concepts i.e. inheritance and polymorphism. With this, we have covered most of the basic as well as advanced Python programming concepts that you will need to develop Python applications. In the next and final chapter, we will study another some other extremely useful tools for programming in Python i.e. Lambda operator and List Comprehensions.

Chapter 14

Lambda Operators and List Comprehensions

In Chapter 11 (Functions in Python) of this book, we studied how we can create lambda functions or anonymous functions in one line of code. However, lambda operator is not merely used to create anonymous functions. There are many other uses of lambda operators which we will study in this chapter.

Mostly, the lambda operator is used in combination with map(), reduce() and filter() operations. We will see the detail of each of these filters in detail, but first let's revise how to create a simple lambda function.

Take a look at a simple example:

```
sum = lambda a,b,c: a + b + c
result = sum(10,15,5)
print(result)
```

In the script above we create a lambda function with three parameters a, b and c. The function adds these three parameters and returns the sum. The function is stored in sum variable. The function can now be called using the sum variable name. We then call the function by passing three numeric arguments to the sum variable and print the result on the screen. The output of the above expression will be 10 + 15 + 5 = 20.

The Map Function

The map function is used to apply a function on a sequence and return updated sequence. The map function takes (1) function to apply as first argument and (2) sequence to be updated as the second argument. The map function returns map type object which can be parsed into list using list function. Take a look at the following example:

```
def takesquare(x):
    return(x * x)


nums = [2,4,6,8,10]


squares    =    map(takesquare,
nums)
print(list(squares))
```

In the script above we create function *takesquare* which takes one parameter and returns square of the value passed as parameter. The function here applies on only one parameter, however using map function, we can apply this function to each individual element of the list. Next in the above script we create a list of even numbers from 2 to 10. Next, we use map function and pass it *takesquare* function as first argument, and the list "nums" as second argument. The map function will apply *takesquare* function on individual element of the list, for instance 2 will be squared to 4, 4 will be squared to 16 and so on. The resultant sequence is stored in the "squares" variable. We then convert the squares object to list and print it on the console. The output will look like this:

```
[4, 16, 36, 64, 100]
```

In the script we did not use lambda function; we simply passed a concrete function. However, the real beauty of map function lies in its ability to use lambda functions. Take a look at the following example:

```
squares2 = map(lambda x: x*x,
nums)
```

```
print(list(squares2))
```

In the script above, we have a map function that uses lambda function to take square of value passed to it and apply this function on the sequence. The output will be similar to that of the previous script:

```
[4, 16, 36, 64, 100]
```

You can even use two or more than two sequences in the map function and apply some functionality on both of the lists, simultaneously. Take a look at the following script:

```
even = [2,4,6,8,10]
odd =  [1,3,5,7,9]
result = map(lambda a,b: a+b, even, odd)
print(list(result))
```

In the script above we have two lists. One contains even numbers from 2 to 10 and the other contains odd numbers from 1 to 7. The map function adds the contents of the list. It is important to mention here that the size of all the sequences in the map function should be equal.

The Filter Function

The filter function also takes two parameters: function and sequence. It returns the items from the sequence for which the function returns true and ignores the remaining items in the sequence. Take a look at a simple example of filter function:

```
nums = [1,2,3,4,5,6,7,8,9,10]
result = filter(lambda a: a %
2 == 0, nums)
print(list(result))
```

In the script above, we have a list of numbers from 1 to 10. In filter function we have a lambda function which returns true if number is divisible by 2. Hence all the even numbers from the nums list will be returned. The output of the script above looks like this:

```
[2, 4, 6, 8, 10]
```

The Reduce Function

The reduce function, like the map and filter functions, take two parameters: function and sequence. However, unlike map and filter functions, the reduce function returns single element. The working of reduce function is simple; it starts by applying the function to the first two elements of the sequence. The function is again applied to the result of the previous function and the third value in the sequence. The process continues until all the values in the sequence are iterated.

This is best explained with the help of an example:

```
from functools import reduce
nums = [2,4,6,8,10]
result = reduce(lambda a,b:
a*b, nums)
print(result)
```

To use reduce function you need to import if first. In the script above the reduce function takes produce of all the even numbers from 2 to 10. The reduce function works by first multiplying 2 and 4. It then multiplies the product of 2 and 4 with the third element i.e. 6 and so on. In the output you will see 3840 i.e. the produce of all the numbers in the nums list.

List Comprehensions

List comprehensions can be used to create lists using set notation. List comprehensions can be used to simplify tasks performed by map and reduce functions. Take a look at a simple example of list comprehension where list of integers is converted into corresponding list of squares of integers.

```
evens = [2,4,6,8,10]
squares = [x*x for x in evens]
print(squares)
```

The above script takes squares of all the even numbers in the evens list and prints them on the console. The output will look like this:

```
[4, 16, 36, 64, 100]
```

Similarly, you can filter items from a list using list comprehension. Take a look at the following example.

```
nums = [1,2,3,4,5,6,7,8,9,10]
evens = [x for x in nums if x % 2 == 0]
print(evens)
```

The script above filters all the even numbers from the nums list and display them on the console.

List comprehensions can also be used to find cross products of two sets of elements. Take a look at the following example:

```
sizes = ['Short', 'Medium', 'Large', 'X-Large' ]
persons = ['Men', 'Women', 'Boy', 'Girl']
cp = [(a,b) for a in sizes for b in persons]
print(cp)
```

In the script above we have two sets in the form of list. The sizes list contains for different sizes while the persons list contains different types of persons. We take the cross product of two lists using list notations and store the result in the "cp" variable which is subsequently printed on the console. The cross product of the sizes and persons list looks like this:

```
[('Short', 'Men'), ('Short', 'Women'), ('Short', 'Boy'), ('Short', 'Girl'), ('Medium', 'Men'), ('Mediu
m', 'Women'), ('Medium', 'Boy'), ('Medium', 'Girl'), ('Large', 'Men'), ('Large', 'Women'), ('Large',
'Boy'), ('Large', 'Girl'), ('X-Large', 'Men'), ('X-Large', 'Women'), ('X-Large', 'Boy'), ('X-Large',
'Girl')]
```

Conclusion and What's Next

In this chapter we completed our discussion on lambda operators and list comprehensions. This chapter marks the end of this book. In this book we studied most of the basic and advanced Python concepts. With these concepts, you should be able to develop any Python applications with the help of different Python libraries. I would suggest that you practice the exercises in this book again and again and then start building small projects like calculator, tic tac toe or hangman game. Remember, you will learn as you program. Happy Coding!!!

William Sullivan

FREE E-BOOK DOWNLOAD :

http://bit.ly/2yJsyq4

or

http://pragmaticsolutionstech.com/

Use the link above to get instant access to the bestselling E-Book **Data Analytics' Guide For Beginners** completely FREE!